Measuring Ireland:

Discerning Values and Beliefs

Edited by Eoin G. Cassidy

VERITAS

Measuring Ireland: Discerning Values and Beliefs

Papers from the Symposium
Measuring Society: Discerning Values and Beliefs – Religion, Culture and the Social Sciences

organised by
The Irish Centre for Faith and Culture (ICFC)

Edited by Eoin G. Cassidy

VERITAS

First published 2002 by
Veritas Publications
7/8 Lower Abbey Street
Dublin 1
Ireland
Email publications@veritas.ie
Website www.veritas.ie

ISBN 1 85390 647 6

Cover design by Bill Bolger
Printed in the Republic of Ireland by Betaprint Ltd, Dublin

*Veritas books are printed on paper made from the wood pulp of
managed forests. For every tree felled, at least one tree is planted, thereby
renewing natural resources.*

Contents

Contributors

Margaret S. Archer is a Professor of Sociology at the University of Warwick. From 1986 to 1990 she was President of the International Sociological Association. She is a founder member of the Pontifical Academy of Social Sciences and sits on its Council. She is also co-director of the Centre for Critical Realism – a registered educational charity.

Michael Breen is Head of Department, Media and Communication Studies, and a joint director of the Centre for Culture, Technology and Values, at Mary Immaculate College, University of Limerick.

Ed Carroll is an independent researcher who has worked collaboratively on projects in the social and cultural sphere. During 2001 he successfully applied to the Irish Youth Foundation to undertake research into the well-being of children related to the National Children's Strategy. Prior to that he spent a year with the Soros Centre for the Arts in Sofia, Bulgaria. Currently, he is working with the EU EQUAL 'Diversity at Work Network'.

Eoin G. Cassidy is Executive Secretary of the Irish Centre for Faith and Culture and Head of the Philosophy Department at the Mater Dei Institute, Dublin City University. He has published widely in the area of faith and culture and is editor of *Faith and Culture in the Irish Context* (Veritas, 1996), and *Prosperity with a Purpose: What Purpose?* (Veritas, 2000).

Tony Fahey is Senior Research Officer with the Economic and Social Research Institute. He has contributed to many publications in the areas of religion and the social sciences.

Tom Inglis is a Senior Lecturer in Sociology in UCD. His research interests are Irish Catholicism, sexuality, the media and adult education. He is author of *Moral Monopoly, Lessons in Irish Sexuality,* and *Religion and Politics.*

Perry Share lectures in Sociology and is Head of the Department of Humanities at the Institute of Technology, Sligo. He is co-author with Hilary Tovey of *A Sociology of Ireland,* published by Gill & Macmillan in 2000, and has published numerous books, articles and conference papers on a range of topics, mainly related to rural society and communication.

David Tuohy is a lecturer in Education in University College Galway, where he specialises in Leadership Administration and Research Methods. His recent publications include books on leadership and strategic planning, research on the points system and *The Inner World of Teaching,* on school culture and teacher development. He is co-author of *Youth 2K – Threat or Promise to a Religious Culture* published by Marino Institute of Education in 2000.

Conor K. Ward is a former Professor of Social Science in UCD. He is the joint author of the report of the ISSP survey on religion published in the December 2000 issue of *Doctrine and Life.*

Acknowledgements

This publication arose out of a symposium entitled *Measuring Society: Discerning Values and Beliefs*, which took place in St Patrick's College Maynooth on 22 and 23 June 2001. It was organised by the ICFC (Irish Centre for Faith and Culture). The editor wishes to acknowledge gratitude to the President of St Patrick's College Maynooth, Msgr Dermot Farrell; Director of the ICFC, Rev. Professor James McEvoy; Mr Philip Furlong, Secretary General, Department of Arts, Heritage, Gaeltacht and the Islands; to all who contributed to the symposium and, in particular, to Ms Breege Lynch whose dedicated work ensured the efficient organisation of the symposium.

Introduction

EOIN G. CASSIDY

Today there is a growing consciousness of the increasing importance of the dialogue between theology and the social sciences. There is an emerging conviction that the Christian religion can both inform as well as be informed by the social sciences in addressing issues of public concern. This raises important considerations as to whether the methodological presuppositions of social sciences exclude a religious/spiritual horizon of meaning and to what extent sociology is capable of measuring religious experience and/or spirituality.

Society and its institutions are increasingly turning to sociologists to inform them as to which social problem ought to be addressed, thus suggesting a more prescriptive rather than descriptive role for a science such as sociology.

- to what extent do the social sciences influence as well as measure the shifts in contemporary Irish culture?
- to what extent do the social sciences have a role in facilitating society to discern issues surrounding values and beliefs?
- to what extent, if at all, can conceptual measurement issues be value free?
- can the social sciences be expected to proffer resolutions for social problems?

- is there an ethical remit in the concern of sociologists with, for example, issues of social exclusion?

Theologians are increasingly turning to the social sciences as a point of entry for dialogue with the contemporary world. In this context, the following questions emerge:

- to what extent do the social sciences provide a critical context within which religious belief patterns are both understood and measured?
- can a Christian ethic inform the work of the social sciences?
- to what extent is there scope for a religious assessment of the issues studied by the social sciences?

This publication has emerged from a symposium organised to explore these issues. Part one entitled *Measuring Ireland: Discerning the Religious Profile of Irish Society* includes four articles that measure religious values and beliefs in contemporary Ireland. In the first of the articles entitled 'Modernity and Religion in Ireland: 1980-2000' I explore the religious beliefs and practices of the Irish people from 1980 to 2000 through the lens of both the International Social Survey Programme (ISSP) and the European Values Study (EVS) surveys. The evidence points to a decline in the moral authority of the Catholic Church, a loss of confidence in the Catholic Church and a decline in religious observance. But despite these changes the Irish remain a deeply religious people with a healthy sense of what is best in the culture of modernity. In the article entitled 'Is Atheism Increasing? Ireland and Europe Compared' Tony Fahey questions the assumption that the Western world is secularised. The focus of his article is on the contemporary religious profile in Ireland and his research is based upon an analysis of the most recent EVS survey material. He is sceptical of the viewpoint that suggests that Ireland is heading towards irreligion or atheism, as the secularisation approach would imply. Rather the analysis suggests that, though there are fewer devout people in Ireland than there were in the past, there has been little by way of a corresponding increase in the numbers of atheists, or whatever one might call those who reject religion outright.

Conor Ward, in an article entitled 'Intimations of Immorality', offers further data upon which to analyse the Irish religious profile today. His article is based on information provided by those interviewed when the ISSP chose religion as the theme for its research in 1998. Ethos is not bounded by territorial limits, so data relating to Ireland is set in the context of data from the other countries of the ISSP. Differences by age groups are also examined. One of the most interesting findings of his analysis is that whilst confidence in churches and religious organisations declined steadily, from the oldest at 59 per cent to 7 per cent of the 18-28 year olds, nevertheless 57 per cent of 18-28 year olds had confidence in their local priest.

The final article in this section is entitled 'Different from their Elders and Betters: Age Cohort Differences in the Irish Data of the European Values Study (EVS) 1999'. From his study of the most recent EVS survey material Michael Breen shows that there are significant differences between age cohorts on social and religious values. However, he acknowledges that it is not clear whether such changes represent a real alternation over time or simply a generational difference. In this respect, further research is both possible and desirable.

Part two entitled *Measuring Society: Discerning the Ethical World of the Social Sciences* includes five articles that reflect upon the presuppositions of the social sciences, the value judgements that social scientists bring to bear upon their work, and some methodological issues that arise from qualitative research. In the first article in this section entitled 'Models of Man Transcendence and Being-in-the-World' Margaret Archer suggests that two 'models of man' have dominated social theory since the Enlightenment, privileging atheism because of their respective anthropocentricism and sociocentrism. These conceptions of 'Modernity's Man' and 'Society's Being' are considered defective for social science and for faith alike. In the article she offers an alternative model from the Realist perspective. In it, what human subjects become derives from the interplay between their biological potentials and their practical interactions with the real world. The second article in this section, written by Tom Inglis, is entitled 'Searching for Truth, Revealing Power, Hoping for Freedom'. In the article he acknowledges that it is hard to get beyond the post-modern notion that truth is produced within discourses that are historically and culturally constituted and which are consequently arbitrary and relative. And yet he insists that for the social scientist there is an interest if not an imperative to search for and announce the truth. As he acknowledges this article is a critical reflection as to how this struggle has been part of his own work as a sociologist. The third article in this section written by Perry Share is entitled 'Food and the Soul: Some Thoughts on the Role of Sociology in Contemporary Ireland'. The article is an attempt to examine the specific connections between social sciences and ethics. This chapter introduces the topic of the sociology of food and outlines how it may connect with ethical issues on the one hand, and different 'styles' of sociology on the other.

From a very different perspective David Tuohy, in an article entitled 'Youth 2K: The Multiple Worlds of Young People', examines some of the issues that have been explored in the earlier articles. The specific focus of his article is on an exploration of some of the issues that arose in interpreting the interview data in a study which he conducted and was subsequently published in a book entitled *Youth 2K: Threat or Promise to a Religious Culture?*. In contrast to the quantitative analysis characteristic of the ISSP and EVS surveys, this study used in-depth interview technique to explore value formation among 17-24 year olds in Ireland. A key focus of the study was on their religious values in the context of other values relating to home, school, work, peers and society in general. The final article in the publication is entitled 'Indicators and Child Well-being: Exploring Conceptual Measurement Issues'. In this article Ed Carroll probes the manner in which the development of indicators can advance a comprehensive understanding of the child. Specifically he is concerned with examining a simple question: namely, how can child well-being be constituted and understood, especially when trying to embed it in the policy, systems and services of government? This is an ethical issue with far reaching implications for the provision of services for children.

PART I

Measuring Ireland: Discerning the Religious Profile of Irish Society

Modernity and Religion in Ireland: 1980-2000

Eoin G. Cassidy

Through an examination of selected surveys, the article looks at the extent to which a number of important features of modernity impacted upon religious beliefs, values and practices in Ireland between 1980 and 2000. In this context, the article analyses the reasons for the decline in the moral authority of the Catholic Church, a loss of confidence in the Catholic Church and a decline in religious observance. The article concludes by observing that by all the standards of international comparison the Irish remain a deeply religious people. They have embraced much of what is good in the culture of modernity without absorbing either an extreme individualism or a form of secularism that blocks access to any transcendent source of meaning.

Introduction

Faith is always transmitted and received in a particular context. Therefore, if one is to have any claims to accurately portray the faith profile of any society one must be sensitive to the cultural parameters within which that faith is lived out. The challenge for any commentator on values and beliefs is to offer a sense of perspective. The difficulty is that there is no neutral vantage point from which to survey any culture. We are all creatures of a particular culture and every culture erects a highly selective screen that makes it difficult to see with clarity our own or any other culture. It is thus with a degree of caution that this article will attempt to explore the extent to which the culture of modernity has affected Irish religious belief patterns over the past twenty years.

It is often said that when Europe was having its revolutions in 1848, events that signalled the close of the Enlightenment, the Irish people were having their famine – a more than slight exaggeration, but one that draws attention to the peculiarity of the Irish situation. The latter half of the nineteenth century and the first half of the twentieth century was a time of dramatic changes in the faith profile of many European countries. In particular, it was a period that saw the virtual collapse in the practice of the faith among much of the European urban working class. At that precise moment Ireland was experiencing a religious revival that had few parallels. It was a religious revival that was to continue to the 1970s. Up until then, the religious profile of Irish society was one that was that bore little relation to our nearest neighbours in Europe, namely an almost universal attendance at religious services and a high degree of acceptance of the moral authority of the Catholic Church.

Times change and the recent changes provide a constant reminder of the folly of presuming that the present is normative. To an outside observer, there is little to parallel the dramatic changes that have marked the Irish faith profile in recent years, changes that have revealed the folly of presuming that Ireland either ever was or would always remain a type of spiritual oasis in an increasingly de-Christianised Europe. To what extent are recent changes in the Irish religious profile over the past twenty to twenty-five years to be understood under the rubric of 'catching up with Europe'? To this end the article will explore recent statistical evidence that casts light on trends in Irish religious belief patterns. Specifically, the article will seek to explore the extent to which the Irish have over the past twenty years embraced those key themes of modernity that have helped to shape the European culture of the present EU states.

In approaching this task one is fortunate to have two series of authoritative surveys that have charted Irish belief patterns in the context of international comparisons. Both the 1991 and 1998 International Social Survey Programme (ISSP)[1] and the 1981, 1990 and 1999 European Values Study (EVS)[2] surveys have done a remarkable job in tracking the changing patterns of Irish beliefs, values and practices over the last twenty years. An analysis of their findings will offer us a valuable opportunity to look at the manner in which modernity is contributing to the changing shape of religious belief in Ireland, because it could be argued that it is only in the last twenty to thirty years that Ireland has emerged from under the shadow of a perceived need to identify Catholicism with nationalism.

Modernity increasingly appears as an umbrella concept for a spectrum of cultural developments that took place in Europe over a period of two hundred years. Four of the core themes that have shaped modernity have been the secularisation of culture, the acceptance of an individualist anthropology, the rise of instrumental reasoning and the development of a liberal culture that flows from an increasing acceptance of liberal democracy. While recognising that these themes by no means fully capture the spirit of modernity, nevertheless, for purposes of space, this article will confine itself to an exploration of the way in which they have impacted on recent Irish faith patterns.

I shall conclude this introduction by offering the briefest of sketches of the four themes which will be explored in the course of this article.

Secularism indirectly has its origins in the rise of secular humanism during the Renaissance in the fifteenth and sixteenth centuries. Its development is, however, closely associated with the rise of the empirical scientific disciplines and the subsequent emergence of a positivist culture. A this-worldly and materialist culture, it denies the existence of any transcendent horizon of meaning. However, the larger movement in culture associated with the term secularisation has no such dogmatic intent. It has given an impetus for a renewed respect for nature and has thus revitalised science in a manner that has brought huge benefits to humankind.

An individualist anthropology can be traced back to the early philosophers of the Enlightenment, but its development is for the most part associated with the emergence of a Protestant ethos in the sixteenth and seventeenth centuries. This cultural development is by its very nature anti-authoritarian and its growth has in no small measure led to the acceptance of a human rights culture. Today it has the potential to create an ethical environment that stresses the importance of self-esteem and the need to be responsible. It also has the potential to enclose itself within the narrow confines of a self-interest that rejects any ties of responsibility to the larger community.

The modern development of a technological world view associated with the rise of instrumental rationality can be traced to the industrial revolution and the rise of capitalism. In its pragmatic concern with efficiency it has promoted a confident self-mastery over our environment. However, the 'can-do' attitude that is typical of a culture that is shaped by the success of instrumental reason could very easily lead to an over-valuing of the logic of the market place, where everything and everybody has a price, to the exclusion of all other values and in particular those associated with a Christian ethic.

Liberalism emerged on the coat tails of the Reformation, a point in European history that marked the break-up of Western Christendom, and with that break-up the loss of a shared understanding of the values, beliefs and practices that define human existence. Five centuries later, the distinguishing feature of a liberal culture continues to be a tolerance of many divergent and in some cases incompatible world-views. From a liberal perspective pluralism is a fact of life, and over the last two hundred years liberal democracies have been developed as a political system that can accommodate pluralism. In this context a liberal culture may inadvertently encourage the acceptance of a relativist ethos that has little sympathy for either the importance of tradition or the belief in the objectivity of moral values. Both of these developments could make it difficult for those who wish to give credence to the teaching role of the moral authority of the Church. A liberal culture can also be expected to foster the idea of an egalitarian ethos in society and the consequent rejection of all forms of authoritarianism. This aspect of liberalism poses a major challenge for an institution such as the Catholic Church that is hierarchically structured.

The Secularisation of Irish Society and the Church's Loss of Moral Authority

Secularisation is the process by which culture progressively defines itself in a 'this-worldly' context, one that in its most radical form, i.e. secularism, excludes any reference to a religious, sacred or transcendent horizon of meaning. This secularisation process is accompanied by the growth of an individualist ethos that encourages a privatisation of core beliefs and values. In attempting to examine the impact of this process on the Irish religious profile it is obviously of first importance to pay attention to any statistics that offer a way of discerning to what extent if any the Irish have begun to adopt a more this-worldly frame of reference. If they are increasingly secularist one would expect this to be reflected in an increase in denominational disaffiliation across all religions, an increasing vagueness in describing belief in God, falling attendances at religious services and a decline in the acceptance of core doctrinal and ethical beliefs associated with any particular religion.

From the most recent statistics (1999 EVS), over 8 per cent of the Irish population can be loosely categorised as 'secularists', in other words they reject any denominational label, Christian or other. Although this figure for 'secularists' remains fairly low by international standards, it has risen appreciably over the past eighteen years; the comparable 1981 EVS figure was only 2.5 per cent.[3] Approximately half of 'secularists' do not believe in God, the others would accept some form of theistic world-view. Over and above those who refuse to be categorised under any denominational label there is a further 1.3 per cent who are Christian but who do not belong to any denomination.[4] In total, over 9 per cent of Irish people do not belong to any religious denomination.

To account for the 1.3 per cent Christians who refused any denominational label one might point to the conflict in Northern

Ireland which has fostered the perception of a link between denominational religion and sectarianism. This may also be a factor in explaining the rise in the figure for 'secularists'. However, a more likely explanation for this figure is the influence of secularising tendencies in Irish culture that contribute both to the increasing privatisation of religious belief and a growing vagueness regarding core religious beliefs.

Over the past three surveys the EVS has measured the extent to which a theistic world-view is anchored in an acceptance of the core Christian understanding of God (Table 1).

Table I

	1981 EVS (All)	1990 EVS (All)	1999 EVS (All)
Belief in God	95%	96%	96%
Belief in a personal God	77%	67%	65%
Belief in some sort of spirit or life force	15%	24%	24%
Don't know	6%	7%	8%
No God or life spirit	2%	1%	3%

The figures reveal a near-universal acceptance of belief in God and one that has remained constant throughout the life-span of the three surveys. However, as we can see, not all those who believe in God would also believe in a personal God. Furthermore, although the decline in belief in a personal God over the past ten years is insignificant the same cannot be said if one extends the analysis over the last eighteen years. The corresponding figure from the 1998 ISSP survey for belief in a personal God is higher at (78 per cent) but still substantially lower than the corresponding figure for belief in God (94 per cent).[5] Looking at the full range of figures there is evidence to suggest an increasingly vague understanding of God. However, in the context of international comparisons the Irish profile remains strongly marked by an adherence to the traditional Christian understanding of a personal God. Of all the countries surveyed about belief in a personal God in the 1998 ISSP survey only the Philippines (88 per cent) scored higher than Ireland (78 per cent).[6] Correspondingly, there are the statistics that show Ireland consistently scoring lowest among 1998 ISSP countries surveyed in terms of belief in such things as good luck charms (24 per cent), fortune-tellers (28 per cent) and horoscopes (19 per cent).

The statistics seem to suggest evidence of a resistance to secularising tendencies at least in comparison to other countries surveyed. Further evidence of this resistance can be found by noting the continued high level of adherence to core religious (Christian) beliefs such as belief in a God, belief in life after death, belief in heaven, hell and sin that are recorded below (Table 2). The high levels of belief in both life after death and heaven suggest the limited appeal of an exclusively materialist philosophy such as secularism. Whether these statistics tell the whole story in regard to the acceptance of core Christian beliefs is, however, debatable because it must also be noted that 20 per cent of those surveyed also believe in re-incarnation.

Although the figures for the youngest age cohort (18-26) are slightly lower, these figures show relatively little variation across age groups. More importantly, it is striking that all of these figures have

Table 2 Acceptance of Core Christian Beliefs

Republic of Ireland

	Belief in God	Belief in life after death	Belief in heaven	Belief in hell	Belief in sin
1981 EVS	95%	76%	83%	54%	85%
1998 ISSP	94%	78%	85%	53%	—
1999 EVS	96%	80%	86%	54%	86%

remained remarkably constant over the eighteen years covered by the surveys. Finally, in terms of international comparison, the Irish figures in all of the above categories are as high if not higher than any other country surveyed by the ISSP.

Further evidence of the limited influence of secularisation in Irish culture can be seen in the 1998 ISSP survey that recorded a high sense of religious identity among the 18-28 age group in Ireland especially among those who had indicated that their religious affiliation was Roman Catholic. This can be illustrated by the fact that 74 per cent of the Irish 18-28 age group expressed belief in 'Christ in the Eucharist' as opposed to an average of 65 per cent for other groups; 64 per cent expressed belief in 'having a Pope as head of the Church' as opposed to an average of 58 per cent for other Irish groups; 68 per cent expressed belief in 'Mary, Mother of Jesus' as opposed to an average of 53 per cent for other Irish groups, while 71 per cent stated they regarded 'Help for the poor' as important as opposed to an average of 62 per cent for other age groups.

The above statistics don't show evidence that the secularisation process has led to a loss of religious identity among a significant percentage of the population or a decline in the acceptance of core beliefs associated with Roman Catholicism. However, this picture changes when we examine the statistics that profile the moral authority of the Roman Catholic Church. There is increasing evidence that Church teaching in key areas of sexual ethics is progressively less influential in determining lifestyle choices among its members or adherents.

As we can see from the figures in Table 3 (p. 25), there is a weakening in adherence to Catholic Church teaching on abortion, pre-marital sexual relations, extra-marital relationships and same sex relationships. In all of these areas the youngest age group (18–26/28) records significantly lower percentage points than all other groups. This suggests a deepening divide between Church teaching and lifestyle choices in this area. There are no easy answers to account for the changing sexual mores evident both in Ireland and throughout Western culture. However, the decline in ethical beliefs associated with

Table 3 Acceptance of key aspects of Roman Catholic Moral Teaching

Irish data over four surveys

	1981 EVS (All)	1990 EVS (All)	1991 ISSP (All)	1998 ISSP (All)	1999 EVS (All)	1998 ISSP (18-28)	1999 EVS (18–26)
Abortion is always wrong	74%	68%	48%	41%	51%	—	30%
Premarital sexual relations are always wrong	—	—	36%	30%	—	8%	—
Extra-marital relationships are always wrong	—	—	71%	63%	72%	43%	56%
Same sex relations are always wrong	—	—	68%	60%	35%	30%	19%

any particular religion that is reflected in these figures does suggest the influence of a secularist ethos. Interestingly, the consistently high number of respondents who refuse to accept the legitimacy of extra-marital relationships suggests a strong resistance to an ethics free-for-all.

Individualism, Secularism and the Privatising of Religious Belief[7]

Whether or not the idea of a secularist culture could ever be separated from the self-understanding of people as individuals, the growth of a secularist mindset in Western societies over the past two centuries has in fact been accompanied by a parallel growth in an individualist anthropology. In the last half-century the two have combined most strikingly in Western societies to effect a widespread decline in social capital. In the context of religious belief this shows itself in the privatisation of religion or the loss of the social dimension of religious belief and practice. To what extent is this trend evident in Ireland?

The figures show a steep decline in attendance at religious services over a ten-year period for all age groups, one that is particularly marked in the figures for the youngest age cohort (Table 4, p. 26).

Table 4   Attendance at Religious Services

Republic of Ireland

Figures in parentheses relate to mass attendance for Catholics

| | Once a week or more | | Once a month or more | |
	All	**18-26 or (28) Age group**	**All**	**18-26 or (28) Age group**
1981 EVS	83% (87%)	75% (79%)	89% (92%)	—
1990 EVS	81% (85%)	71% (76%)	78% (83%)	—
1998 ISSP	63%	33%	73%	53%
1999 EVS	59% (65%)	23%	70%	48%

However, this 'decline' must be seen in the larger context of religious practice in the Western world (Table 5, p. 27). When comparisons are made with other surveyed countries one sees a slightly different picture.

Attendance at religious services in Ireland is remarkably high by international comparison. One still has to seek to explain the decline in the Irish figures, but in the light of international comparisons the more appropriate question to ask is how can one explain the exceptionally high attendance figures that marked the Irish religious profile for most of the twentieth century rather than to look for reasons for the decline from this high plateau.

In the light of an examination of attendance at religious ceremonies there is another series of figures that are worth showing. Table 6 (p. 27) examines the importance attached to religious ceremonies associated with birth, marriage and death.

Table 5   International Frequencies of Church Attendance

Two or three times a month or more often

ISSP 1998

Country	Frequency*
Republic of Ireland	73%
Switzerland	64%
Poland	62%
Northern Ireland	51%
Italy, Slovakia, Portugal	44%-41%
USA, Chile, Spain, Austria	39%-33%
Norway, Cyprus, Denmark, Sweden, Russia, and Japan	Below 10%

*Countries listed in descending order

Table 6   Importance attached to Religious Services

1999 EVS Survey: Republic of Ireland

	Birth	Marriage	Death
All	91%	93%	96%
25–34 age group	88%	87%	93%

These figures show strong evidence not only of a high sense of religious sensibility among Irish people when marking the important moments of their lives but also of the almost universal desire to publicly celebrate these events with religious services. The figures contained in these last two tables ought make one wary of exaggerating the increasing privatisation of religious beliefs and practices.

One way of measuring the religious sensibility of the Irish population is to look at the figures on the frequency of prayer in people's lives and the extent to which they find comfort and support in prayer. On a very different level, an examination of these figures might also assist in measuring the growth of a privatisation of religion. Outside of the context of a communal celebration, prayer is by its very nature a private affair. If the decline in attendance at religious services is not replicated in figures that show a decline in the frequency of prayer in people's lives, one might have evidence that suggests a decrease in a belief in a communal context for the celebration of religious belief rather than any decline in religious belief itself.

Both the 1998 ISSP and the 1999 EVS surveys measured the frequency of prayer in people's lives. As we can see from Table 7 (below) the figures recorded by the two surveys were not identical. Looking at the percentage figure for praying several times a week the ISSP figure at (45 per cent) is considerably lower than the comparable EVS figure at (60 per cent).

Table 7   Frequency of Personal Prayer
Ireland: Across all ages

Figures in parentheses relate to Catholics

	1999 EVS	1998 ISSP
Every day	46%	–
Several times a week	60% (66%)	45%
Once a week	70%	70%

In terms of international comparison the ISSP survey figures place Ireland in the top third of the countries surveyed. However, the Irish figure at 45 per cent is considerably lower than that recorded in the Philippines (80 per cent) and the USA (60 per cent). It is also marginally lower than that recorded in Northern Ireland (46 per cent). At the other end of the scale, the percentage who said that they never prayed was lowest in the Philippines (0 per cent) followed by Ireland at

5 per cent. The comparison with Ireland's nearest neighbours is as follows: Northern Ireland (17 per cent) and Great Britain (35 per cent).

A more valuable barometer of the importance of prayer in people's lives is to be found in answer to the question as to whether one draws comfort and strength from prayer. The 1981 EVS reported a figure of (80 per cent) and the 1990 EVS a figure of (82 per cent). In neither survey did the figure for any age group fall below 64 per cent. In answer to the corresponding question in the 1999 EVS survey as to whether one draws comfort and strength from religion, 76 per cent across all ages said yes with only the 18–26 age group (54 per cent) having a figure of less than 60 per cent. The 1999 EVS figures for Catholics in the Republic and Northern Ireland are ROI (80 per cent) and NI (85 per cent) respectively.

The importance attached to prayer would seem to offer clear evidence of the limited appeal of a secularist mindset. When one compares the continual high figures in answer to the question as to whether one draws comfort and strength from prayer or religion with the decline in the figures for attendance at religious services a slightly different picture emerges, one that suggests evidence for an increasing privatising of religious belief. The statistics do not say that the Irish are not religious but rather that when it comes to giving expression to their beliefs they increasingly prefer a private to a communal setting.

Preserving Social Capital in an Individualist Culture

One way of measuring the growth of an individualist culture is to see to what extent people espouse the positive ideal or ethic of authenticity, one that shows itself in the importance that people attach to values such as 'self-esteem', 'self worth', 'realising one's own potential', or 'being true to oneself'. Over the course of the EVS surveys there were a number of questions that touched on these individualist values. One of the most interesting measured respondents' answers when asked to choose five qualities that children can be encouraged to learn at home:

Table 8   Qualities which children can be encouraged to learn at home
EVS 1999
Listed in order of importance

Good manners	87%
Tolerance and respect for other people	75%
Feeling of responsibility	54%
Independence	50%
Unselfishness	50%
Obedience	48%
Religious faith	39%
Hard work	37%
Determination and perseverance	28%
Imagination	24%
Thrift, saving money and things	23%

From these figures and those in Table 9 (below) there is clear evidence that over a ten-year period there has been an increase in Irish people's sense of themselves as individuals and an acceptance of the importance of the liberal ethic of tolerance and good manners. Two key indicators of an individualist ethos, independence and responsibility, are very highly valued. The same cannot be said for determination and perseverance which, although showing higher figures in the most recent of the surveys, is doing so from a very low base. To explain this discrepancy one might imagine reluctance on the part of the respondents to stress determination and perseverance for fear that this might put too much pressure on children.

Table 9   Qualities which children can be encouraged to learn at home
EVS   Comparison over three surveys

	1981 EVS	1990 EVS	1999 EVS
Valuing independence	30%	43%	50%
Valuing responsibility	22%	61%	54%
Valuing determination and perseverance	10%	26%	28%

In extreme forms of individualism the positive appropriation of oneself as an individual can be accompanied by a withdrawal from engagement with the community. In popular literature individualism is often so portrayed and thus is seen as a trend that is inimical to the promotion of important societal goals that flow from Christian social teaching. By providing evidence of the extent to which Irish people are involved with voluntary organisations, the EVS survey offers us a good way to measure the social capital of Irish society, the commitment of Irish people to social goals, and thus to analyse the extent to which, if at all, extreme individualism has a hold on the Irish psyche (Table 10).

Table 10	Participation in voluntary organisations in Ireland	
	1990 EVS (All)	1999 EVS (All)
Membership of at least one voluntary organisation	49%	57%
Work for at least one voluntary organisation	27%	33%

The figures offer no evidence of the increasing influence of extreme individualism. If anything the opposite is the case. Furthermore, in terms of international comparisons Ireland is in the top third of European countries measured by the EVS[8] a figure that suggests that one would be unwise to exaggerate the influence of an extreme form of individualism on Irish societal mores. This hesitancy is reinforced when one takes account of other figures from the 1999 EVS survey. In a set of questions respondents were asked about their willingness to give practical expression to their concerns by indicating their 'willingness to help' various groups in society. This was recorded on a five-point scale (1: absolutely 'yes' to 5 absolutely 'no'). Family, neighbours, the elderly, the sick and the disabled all received a score of 2 or under (a strong willingness to help) across all age groups. The only category of people that did not seem to receive that type of support were immigrants who received a score of 2.8 (close to the response 'maybe yes, maybe no'), with very little variation across age groups.

Overall, there is evidence that Irish people possess a high level of social capital. Furthermore, there is very little difference across age groups in Ireland when it comes to measuring the level of concern for others. This suggests that any lack of social concern among Irish people cannot be attributed to recent changes in culture since one would expect any such changes to have the greatest influence on the youngest age group.

Capitalism, Individualism and the Pursuit of Instrumental Rationality

The rise of individualism is often linked to that of capitalism. In fact, many would argue that capitalism as an indicator of a cultural ethos as well as an economic theory would never have successfully inserted itself into the cultural fabric of contemporary Western society if it were not for the rise of an individualist anthropology in the seventeenth and eighteenth centuries. Whatever about the merits of the argument it is undoubtedly true that capitalism is an individualist doctrine that in its extreme forms divides the world into winners and losers. Individualist capitalism that embraces the logic of market forces has been in the ascendancy in Western society since the 1980s. To what extent have Irish people adopted this cultural theory that clearly is at odds with the core social teachings of the Christian faith? Over the past three EVS surveys an impressive amount of data has be gathered that charts the shifting balance between left and right leaning economic views of Irish society. The 1990 analysis of the data suggested that 40 per cent of Irish society had left leaning economic views, roughly comparable to the European average of 43 per cent.[9] The 1999 EVS figures (Table 11, p. 33) that trace responses to the question as to why there are people in Ireland who live in need offers a way of measuring the current position.

Measuring the preferences given to 'laziness or lack of will power' on the one hand and 'injustice in society' on the other, offer us one

Table 11　　　　**Reasons why people in Ireland live in need**　*1999 EVS*
The figures in parentheses show the second reason given by respondents

	18 – 26	All other ages combined	Total
Because they were unlucky	20% (20%)	24% (26%)	23% (25%)
Because of laziness or lack of will power	16% (22%)	23% (19%)	21% (19%)
Because of injustice in society	36% (16%)	32% (25%)	33% (23%)
An inevitable part of modern progress	19% (37%)	19% (27%)	19% (29%)
None of these	8% (5%)	3% (3%)	4% (4%)

way of measuring classic left and right leaning economic views of Irish society. As presented the figures don't provide any evidence of the increasing influence of an individualist and/or capitalist logic. Interestingly, it is the youngest cohort surveyed that gave most credence to 'injustice in society'. One would have imagined that this cohort would have been most susceptible to capitalism's increasing profile. This is obviously not the case.

Another set of figures from the 1999 EVS survey broadly confirms the above picture. In answer to the question as to whether one would choose freedom or equality (the classical expression of the right/left distinction) there was a slight overall preference for freedom (48 per cent) over equality (45 per cent). However, in line with what was observed above, this picture is reversed in the 18-26 age cohort where the preference figure for freedom is (41 per cent) and that for equality is (52 per cent).

Finally, in answer to the 1999 EVS series of questions asking respondents to rate themselves on various issues, respondents showed a strong attachment to individual freedom and responsibility, one that offers confirmation of a continuation of the trends towards a healthy valuing of oneself as an individual that we observed in the 1981 and 1990 EVS statistics above. In choosing between the following; (a)

'Individuals should take more care of themselves' and (b) 'The state should take more responsibility to ensure that everyone is provided for' there was a clear preference across all ages for (a). On a scale of 1-10, 35 per cent of all respondents and 37 per cent of the 18-26 age cohort placed a very high emphasis (1-3) on individual responsibility. Similarly, when asked whether competition is good or harmful, 47 per cent of all respondents thought it was very good (a 1-3 rating), and the similar rating figure for the 18–26 age cohort was 54 per cent. Finally, in the choice between (a) 'Incomes should be made more equal' and (b) 'There should be greater incentives for individual effort' there was a clear preference for (b). On a scale of 1-10, 38 per cent of all respondents and 36 per cent of the 18–26 age cohort emphasised (1-3) that there should be greater incentives for individual effort.

Overall on the basis of the figures, there is evidence that the Irish have a healthy respect for themselves as individuals together with an acceptance of both the freedom and responsibility that accompanies one's self-acceptance as an individual. However, there is no evidence of either an extreme individualism or the whole-scale adoption of a capitalist logic, both of which promote a disengagement from the sense of one belonging to a community or having responsibility for the health of the community where one lives.[10]

Liberalism, Liberal Democracy and the Pursuit of an Anti-authoritarian Agenda

To embrace the cultural ethos of liberalism is to embrace a culture that gives recognition to the individual. In that context, many of the themes that we have discussed above could just as easily have been treated under this present heading. However, in this section I want to look primarily at a key theme of modernity, namely the related ideals of an egalitarian society and the rejection of authoritarianism, a theme that flows from the acceptance of liberal democracy and a culture of liberalism. Furthermore, I want to examine the extent to which this cultural development impacts on the acceptance of religious values and beliefs in Ireland today. We have already briefly examined some of the statistics that make reference to the ideal of equality and the figures suggest that the Irish are by no means insensitive to the importance of aspiring to an egalitarian society. It remains to reflect on the issue of authoritarianism.

Authoritarianism can be defined as 'a collective disposition to defer to those in positions of authority'.[11] Three ways of measuring the extent of authoritarianism in Ireland were suggested in the commentary on the 1990 EVS survey: (a) the answer to the question as to whether a greater emphasis on authority would be a good thing, (b) the priority given to protecting freedom of speech over maintaining order in the nation, and (c) the extent to which the respondents believe that there can be absolutely clear guidelines about what is good and evil.[12] Table 12 (below) examines the extent of authoritarianism in Ireland using these three measurement guides.

Table 12 **Authoritarianism in Ireland**
Percentage agreeing

	EVS 1990 (All)	European average 1990 (All)	EVS 1999 (All)
Greater respect for authority a good thing	83%	57%	75%
Protection of free speech a priority	42%	51%	34%
There are absolutely clear guidelines about what is good and evil	45%	39%	39%
Greater emphasis on the development of the individual is a good thing	—	—	89%

The survey response to the question on ethical guidelines suggests a loss of confidence in the capacity of the churches or any other institution to provide moral leadership. This could be evidence of an increase in a relativist and/or a sceptical stance regarding the existence of the Good or the good life. A loss of confidence in the objectivity and intelligibility of the Good was one of the key developments that gave rise to the pluralist ethos characteristic of a liberal society. In this limited but important area there is evidence of an increasing acceptance of a liberal ethos. However, this cannot be said regarding either of the two other measures of authoritarianism. Respect or deference to authority remains exceptionally high and the priority that the respondents would accord to that key characteristic of liberal democracy, namely freedom of speech, has actually fallen over the course of the past ten years. How then to explain the extremely high priority attached to the development of the individual that I have included in this table? It is a figure that would seem to be at odds with any undue deference to authority. It would be rash to presume on the basis of these figures that the Irish have a collective disposition to defer to those in authority. Responses to another series of questions in the 1999 EVS survey reinforce this hesitancy. In answer to a question about one's preferences for running the country both the idea of a strong leader who was not democratically accountable (25 per cent), or the choice of having experts rather than government make decisions (34 per cent), or the choice of the army to rule the country (4 per cent), fared very low on people's preferences compared with the choice of having a democratic political system (85 per cent).

How does the growth of an egalitarian and anti-authoritarian society impact on the profile of religion in Ireland? It might be expected that a liberal culture which embraces the ideals of equality and individual freedom would have little confidence in a hierarchically structured Church that is perceived by some as not doing enough to foster either a participative culture or an egalitarian ethos. There are a number of questions in both the ISSP and EVS surveys that probe the issue of confidence in the Church.

A comparison between the ISSP surveys of 1991 and 1998 offers evidence that there has been a loss of confidence in the Church and religious organisations. The 1991 ISSP figure for 'complete confidence or great deal of confidence' in the Church and religious organisations is 46 per cent whereas the corresponding 1998 figure is 28 per cent. Furthermore, the same statistics for 1998, analysed by age groups, show a steady decline from a confidence level of 59 per cent from the oldest age cohort (over 69 years of age) to the extremely low figure of 7 per cent from the youngest age cohort (18-28 years of age).

Perhaps the most revealing statistic to emerge from the ISSP survey is that Irish people's confidence in religious leadership and the Church as an institution has decreased during a period when confidence in other institutions such as parliament, the legal system and the educational system has either increased or remained static. Furthermore, as we see below, data relating to confidence in the Church as an organisation placed the Republic of Ireland in the lower half of the league table of countries surveyed.

Table 13   **Complete or great deal of confidence in the Church as an Organisation (1998 ISSP)**

Country	Frequency*
Philippines	72%
Chile	54%
Cyprus, USA, Portugal, Slovakia, Hungary, Poland	44%-40%
Russia, Latvia, Spain, Denmark, **Northern Ireland**, Italy, Australia, Norway	39%-31%
Israel, **Republic of Ireland**, Canada, Austria, Former West Germany, Switzerland, Slovenia, The Netherlands, Bulgaria, New Zealand, Sweden	28%-21%
Great Britain, Former East Germany, Czech Republic, France	17%-13%

The EVS surveys have also measured confidence in the Church and the figures confirm the dramatic loss of confidence particularly in the Catholic Church in the Republic of Ireland over the course of the life-span of the three surveys (Table 14).

Table 14   Declining Confidence in the Church among regular church attenders
Republic of Ireland and Northern Ireland
EVS 1981 – 1999

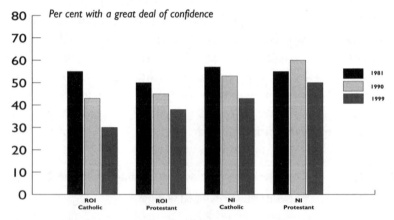

Note: Regular church attenders are people who reported that they were Catholic or Protestant and said they attended religious services at least once a month
ROI = Republic of Ireland   NI = Northern Ireland

One of the most valuable barometers of confidence is to be seen in Table 15 (p. 39) which charts the manner in which people have responded to the question as to whether the Church gives adequate answers in areas within which it would claim a competency. In all categories the figures show evidence of a significant decline in confidence in the Church. It is only in the area of addressing people's spiritual needs that the figure for confidence in the Church is higher than 50 per cent.

One of the most interesting findings of the 1998 ISSP survey is the evidence of a marked contrast, across all ages, between confidence in the Church and religious organisations at 28 per cent and the local

Priests/Clergy at 42 per cent. Furthermore, in the same survey, Table 16 (below), there is striking evidence of a high level of confidence in the local priest, particularly among the 18-28 age group. Even where these figures are lowest they are still significantly higher than those recorded for confidence in the Church and religious organisations.

Table 15   Confidence in the Church |

Does the Church (Churches) give adequate answers: Answer yes %	1981 EVS (All)	1990 EVS (All)	1999 EVS (All)
To the moral problems and the needs of the individual?	53%	42%	31%
To the problems of family life?	48%	35%	27%
To people's spiritual needs	66%	71%	58%
To the social problems facing the country	—	34%	24%

Table 16   Attitude towards local clergy
Data from ISSP 1998

Confidence in local clergy	Ireland 18–28 Age group	Ireland 48–58 Age group
Female	53%	30%
Male	59%	40%

These figures suggest that in Ireland there is a higher level of identification with the local church community than with the Church as a national or universal institution. Furthermore, there is evidence to suggest that there is a link between the high sense of Catholic identity among young people and the evidence of the strong sense of confidence that the youngest age cohort surveyed would seem to have in the local priest.

To explain the strong sense of Catholic identity in Ireland, particularly evident in the youngest age cohort, one has to recognise that a culture that encourages independence and self-reliance and that prioritises creativity over tradition is also one that can give rise to a loss of any sense of belonging to a community. This in turn can foster a sense of rootlessness and a desire to find anchor points in a tradition that offers both a sense of purpose to life alongside membership of a community. The evidence of a high level of confidence in the local clergy reflects credit on them but it is also evidence of the importance that the local community can play in the life of young people today. It can provide a counter-balance to an excessive individualist ethos.

Concluding Assessment

Looking at the Irish faith profile through the lens of these surveys there is no doubting the evidence of a growth in the secularisation of Irish society and the increasing acceptance of the main tenets of liberalism such as an individualist anthropology and a pluralist ethical environment. However, this study should caution us not to exaggerate the extent to which Ireland has uncritically adopted all expressions of modernity. The increasing acceptance of liberalism should not blind us to the continuing high level of respect for authority that was noted in the surveys. Similarly, the evidence of a growth in an individualist anthropology cannot be translated into an exaggerated form of individualism that rejects all ties to community that are not founded on pure self-interest. The high level of social capital reflected in the strong links that bind Irish people to their community and the evidence of a clear recognition of social inclusion suggest that Ireland is far from uncritically buying into either the logic of individualist capitalism or the pure pragmatism of instrumental reasoning.

To what extent does the analysis of the data from these surveys over eighteen years suggest that the growing influence of modernity on Irish cultural mores has negatively impacted on religion? There is clear evidence of a significant decline in three key areas of religious beliefs and practices, namely, the belief in the moral authority of the Church, attendance at religious services, and confidence in the Catholic Church in the Republic of Ireland. There is also evidence of a consistent growth, albeit from a very small base, in the number of those 'secularists' who refuse any attachment to denominational religion whether Christian or not. Finally, there is evidence of a continuing high level of ethical relativism that is suggested by a growing scepticism regarding the possibility of obtaining clear guidelines from the Church or any other body about what constitutes good and evil.

However, that is by no means the whole picture. For instance, there is little if any evidence of the growth in the secularisation of Irish society leading to a loss of a sense of the spiritual or to a decline in either the belief in traditional core Christian doctrines or the sense of the importance of God, religion or prayer in the lives of Irish people. Furthermore, there are no clear grounds for believing that either a consumerist or an instrumentalist culture has as yet succeeded in undermining people's attachment to a religious and ethical ideal such as fidelity in a relationship. Finally, one can point to the development of a healthy individualism that promotes an ethic of authenticity or a culture of responsibility. One can also point to the rejection of extreme individualism that was observed in the survey that suggests a continuing commitment to the core social character of Christian living. In short, all the evidence points to the fact that while accepting many key tenets of modernity the Irish remain a deeply religious people with an increasing sense of responsibility towards themselves and towards others.

Before concluding this article I wish to revisit those areas in the Irish religious profile that registered the most serious decline over the lifetime of the surveys, namely belief in the moral authority of the Catholic Church, attendance at religious services, and confidence in the Catholic Church particularly in the Republic of Ireland. How are we to assess the reasons for this decline and to what extent will understanding these reasons assist those concerned with meeting the challenges facing religious belief for the coming generation?

Unfortunately, none of the surveys directly asked respondents to comment upon reasons for their responses in any of these three areas. Nevertheless, the statistics do provide us with evidence with which to make an assessment, albeit one that it is inevitably tentative.

It is clear from the statistics over the past twenty years that the pattern of almost universal acceptance in the Irish Catholic tradition of weekly attendance at mass is gone, at least for the foreseeable future. There are no easy answers to account for this change in religious practice. As mentioned above, it may be an instance of a wider move to a more privatised form of religious belief that accompanies an individualist and secular culture. It may also be simply that people no longer rely on the Sunday sermon for news or opinions, or that the symbolism of the liturgy no longer communicates with large segments of the urban population, or that the secular aspects of Sunday are served in some other way. Alternatively, one might point to the influence in contemporary Western culture of a consumerist ethos that favours novelty over tradition, a cultural factor that clearly has an appreciable influence on the youngest age cohort.

All of these factors have undoubtedly contributed in some measure to the decline in mass attendance figures. However, what is increasingly becoming clear is that the high levels of attendance recorded in the century and a half up until the 1980s were not typical and that the present 'decline' is from an artificially high base. While not wishing to downplay the religious reasons for the very high attendance figures over this period there were obviously other factors at play. The increasing political imperative in post-famine Ireland to assert an identity separate to that of Britain necessitated the cultivation of distinctive symbols of Irishness. In this context, with the progressive decline of the Irish language, it became increasingly important both politically and culturally to stress that other great badge of Irish identity, namely the Catholic religion. It is only in recent years that this particular badge of Irish identity has become largely redundant. With a shared political agenda in the EU and the increasing cooperation between the governments over Northern Ireland, the political and cultural imperative is no longer to stress that which separates us but rather that which unites us. In this changed cultural environment the link between Irishness and Catholicism is increasingly perceived as anachronistic and a key cultural factor that encouraged high attendance figures at mass no longer applies.

How do we account for the decline in the moral authority of the Catholic Church? One can certainly point to a very changed cultural environment not only in Ireland but also throughout the Western world that makes it difficult for the Catholic Church's teaching, particularly in the area of sexual morality, to find a ready acceptance. How to account for the changing sexual mores evident both in Ireland and throughout Western culture? Clearly there are socio-economic factors at work that contribute to this new environment. These would include the changing demographic, economic and work patterns in the industrialised world. The increasingly pluralist and relativist moral environment in which we live and which were observed in the surveys is obviously another factor to be taken into account when seeking to understand this changed cultural environment. Also, one should not underestimate the influence of instrumental reasoning, that exclusive concern with pragmatic effectiveness that is increasingly seen to provide the only parameters within which all transactions and relationships are understood. In such an environment ethics has no place. Although there is evidence in the Irish data of a resistance to this consumerist ethic, where everything and everyone has a shelf life, one would be foolish to ignore its presence.

How to account for the loss of confidence in the Catholic Church? For those concerned to promote religious beliefs and values in Ireland this is the most serious issue to be addressed. When one takes into account both that the Irish have the highest level of trust in public institutions in Europe and that there has been no comparable decline in public confidence in other public institutions, the decline in confidence in the Catholic Church in the Republic of Ireland is quite dramatic. Clearly, the sex abuse scandals, which have recently come into the public forum, and the manner in which they were perceived to have been handled, have been a factor in the loss of confidence in the Catholic Church. However, the evidence of the establishment over the past ten years in Ireland of a multitude of tribunals is a reminder that the Catholic Church is not the only public body that has had to face its scandals. Yet it is the Catholic Church in the Republic of Ireland that has suffered the steepest decline in confidence, a decline which had become evident a full decade before the furore over the scandals erupted.

The reasons for this increasing alienation from the institutional Church in Ireland have not yet been properly articulated. It may be that the high level of confidence recorded up until the early 1980s was not typical and that therefore this 'decline' is from an artificially high plateau. It may also be that Catholic Church authority has waned, that people are no longer ruled by fear of the afterlife, or that the Catholic Church's teaching on social and sexual ethics is perceived as outmoded. However, there may be another cultural factor at play, namely the increasing influence of Liberalism and a liberal democratic culture that at least in theory is wedded to the ideals of a participatory and egalitarian society. It is a cultural reality that poses real difficulties for anyone trying to understand and accept the hierarchical structure of Church. Until relatively recently, hierarchical structures governed most aspects of Irish and indeed Western society. Times change. Today any society or organisation that is not perceived to encourage an egalitarian and participative ethos may increasingly be regarded as ethically suspect.

To what extent the decline in confidence in the institutional character of the Catholic Church can be attributed to a perceived failure on its part to promote an egalitarian and participative Church structure is hard to judge. However, the contrast with the high levels of confidence in the local clergy and the local church community might suggest that confidence is higher in surroundings that encourage a participative ethos. If this assessment is correct the challenge facing the Catholic Church is to break a perceived link between Church authority and the acceptance of an authoritarian ethos.

Notes

1. I wish to acknowledge the permission of Professor Conor Ward to reproduce statistics from the ISSP Surveys.
2. I wish to acknowledge the permission of the ESRI to reproduce statistics from the 1999 EVS Survey.
3. The corresponding figures for secularists in Northern Ireland are 1981 EVS (3.5%) and 1999 EVS (14%). The very high NI figures compared with the ROI figures can be accounted for by the fact that most 'secularists' come from a Protestant background.
4. Those who answered 'yes' to the question 'Do you belong to a religious denomination?' and who answered 'Christian (no denomination)' when asked to name the religious denomination to which they belonged. (V102)
5. The question in the 1998 ISSP survey was as follows: 'There is a God who concerns himself with every human being personally, do you agree?'
6. The figure for Northern Ireland (66%) reflects the high level of those with no affiliation to any denomination, Christian or other (14% EVS 1999). For the most part these were formerly members of one of the Protestant denominations.
7. For a detailed treatment of the concept of the theme of individualism see my article 'Religion and Culture: The Freedom to be an Individual' in Eoin G. Cassidy (ed.) *Faith and Culture in the Irish Context* (Dublin, Veritas, 1996), pp. 55-69.
8. The comparative figures for Northern Ireland are as follows: Membership of at least one voluntary organisation, 1990 (56%), 1999 (46%); those who do work for at least one voluntary organisation, 1990 (26%), 1999 (21%).
9. See Niamh Hardiman and Christopher Whelan, 'Values and Political Partnership' in C. Whelan (ed.) *Values and Social Change in Ireland* (Dublin, Gill and Macmillan, 1994), p. 163.
10. For a more detailed treatment of this theme see Eoin G. Cassidy (ed.), *Prosperity with a Purpose: What Purpose? Papers from the Conference Economics, Values and the Common God, organised by the Irish Centre for Faith and Culture* (Dublin, Veritas, 2000).
11. N. Hardiman and C. Whelan, 'Politics and Democratic Values' in C. Whelan (ed.), *Values and Social Change in Ireland* (Dublin, Gill and Macmillan, 1994), p. 123.
12. *ibid.* 126-7.

Is Atheism Increasing?
Ireland and Europe Compared

TONY FAHEY

In the face of widespread instances where churches continue to thrive and abundant evidence of some form of religious orientation even in those countries where participation in church religion is low, how accurate is the assumption that the Western world is secularised? In an examination of survey evidence on religious practice and belief in Ireland today this chapter questions the assumption that Ireland is heading towards irreligion or atheism, as the secularisation approach would imply. Rather the analysis suggests that though there are fewer devout people in Ireland than there were in the past, there has been little by way of a corresponding increase in the numbers of atheists, or whatever one might call those who reject religion outright. Despite the scaling down of formal religious practice, the vast majority of people continue to believe in God, to consider themselves religious, and to think it important to have religious ceremonies at births, marriages and deaths.

Introduction

Religion, it would seem, is in retreat in Ireland. Church attendance is falling, priests and religious are becoming scarcer, scandals involving the clergy and hierarchy abound, and public policy on the family and sexual morality is now shaped with little reference to church teaching.

It would also seem that, in moving in this direction, Ireland is simply falling into line with broad international trends. Secularisation and modernity are usually regarded as so much a part of each other that Ireland appears odd for having remained so religious for so long rather than for showing a fall-off in recent years.

However, recent scholarship in the sociology of religion has begun to challenge the received wisdom on these issues and to portray a different context within which trends in religious attachment in Ireland might be viewed.[1] For one thing the presumed dominance of secularisation has been challenged by evidence of widespread instances where churches continue to thrive. The 'American exception' is one such instance. Some churches in the United States have declined, but many others have expanded, and the overall level of religious attachment is not only high by comparison with Europe but also has remained more or less unchanged since the nineteenth century.[2] In addition, there have been some indications of revival in church affiliation and attendance in post-communist eastern Europe, though the import of these indications is as yet unclear.[3] Apart from these cases of vitality in churchly religion, there is abundant evidence of broader durability in some forms of religious orientation even among those people and in those countries where participation in church religion has become very low. People in such situations may no longer go to church but they continue to hold on to many aspects of traditional religious orientations, such as a general belief in the existence of God, the occasional practice of prayer, and a search for consolation in religion at times of crisis in their lives. In the light of these patterns, there are many who would say that abandonment of organised churchly religion does not signify a move to irreligion but rather an informalisation and privatisation of religion, and its consequent transfer from the public realm into the realm of private feeling and belief.

The purpose of the present chapter is to examine survey evidence on religious practice and belief in Ireland today in order to see which of these accounts of present-day trends in religiosity best reflects the Irish experience. The evidence is looked at in a broader European comparative framework, since that provides us with benchmarks against which Irish patterns can be judged. The concern in part is to establish how far traditional forms of religiosity have declined, but also to explore what, if anything, is emerging in their place. Is Ireland heading towards irreligion or atheism, as the secularisation approach would imply? Or are there indications of underlying persistence in religious attachment, even if the forms of that attachment may be changing, as the critics of the secularisation thesis argue?

The data used here to answer these questions are drawn from the surveys carried as part of the 1999-2000 European Values Study. The 1999-2000 EVS is a Europe-wide survey of values and attitudes which was previously carried out in western European countries in 1981 and 1990.[4] The novelty of the 1999-2000 survey is that it expanded to include much of central and eastern Europe as well as western Europe, covering a total of thirty-three countries. The evidence on religious belief and practice from this source is looked at here under two broad headings. The first is attachment to institutional religion as measured by three indicators – church membership, church attendance and confidence in the church. The second is informal or privatised religion, as measured by a range of indicators of respondents' orientations to forms of religiosity which do not require active participation in a particular church or denomination.

Church Membership
A basic indicator of churchly religiosity is given by survey respondents' willingness to identify themselves as members of a particular church or denomination. Data on this question is given for the thirty-three European societies in the 1999-2000 EVS in Figure 1 (p. 49).

These data show that only 9 per cent of the adult population in Ireland have disavowed church membership entirely. This is low by European standards, though four societies – Iceland, Poland, Greece and Malta – are lower still. Broadly speaking, levels of disaffiliation are somewhat higher in former communist Europe than in the established west European democracies, but the differences are neither as wide nor as consistent as might be expected. The highest levels of disaffiliation

Figure 1   **Adults with no religious affiliation, European countries, 1999-2000**

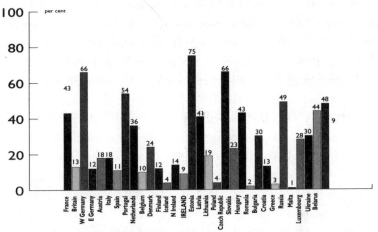

are found in three former communist societies – East Germany, Estonia and the Czech Republic, each of which has over 60 per cent of adults who do not belong to any church – but the next highest level is found in the Netherlands (55 per cent), while France, Belgium and Sweden are in broadly the same range as the majority of the former communist countries. Nevertheless, disaffiliation from church is considerably less common in western than in eastern Europe: twelve west European societies had levels of disaffiliation from church below 20 per cent compared to only four former communist countries (Latvia, Poland, Romania and Croatia). (No data were available for Britain on this item in the 1999-2000 EVS, though data from elsewhere indicate that about 45 per cent of the British population indicate they have no churchly affiliation – Hayes 2000).

Figure 2 (p. 50) gives an indication of trends in churchly disaffiliation by comparing levels in 1999-2000 with those in the 1990 EVS for the countries that were included in both surveys. In no case is the shift in levels of disaffiliation over the 1990s very large but in all cases bar one (Portugal) it is in the same direction – upwards. In

Ireland, the increase in this period was from 4 per cent to 9 per cent. This is a large relative increase, but is modest in absolute terms. It also contradicts the idea that scandals afflicting the Catholic church in Ireland in the 1990s are likely to have caused widespread departures among former believers. Looking at Europe as a whole, then, levels of disaffiliation from churches are very diverse. One cannot say that Ireland fits into, or fails to fit into, any underlying standard pattern on this dimension, since no such standard pattern seems to exist.

Figure 2.   **Adults with no religious affiliation in 1990 and 1999**

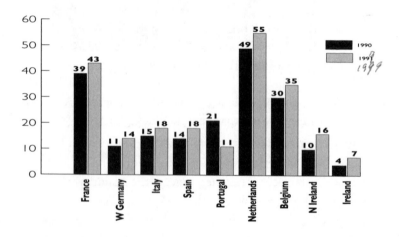

Church Attendance

We now turn to the most widely used indicator of attachment to organised religion – church attendance. Findings based on this indicator need to be read with caution since doubt has been cast on the reliability of self-reported data on church attendance.[5] In the United States, for example, Presser and Stinson (1998) cite evidence which suggests that over-reporting of church attendance in interviewer based surveys has risen steadily since the 1960s, mainly because of social desirability bias (the tendency of respondents to give interviewers the answers they think the interviewers would prefer to hear). Presser and Stinson estimate that actual church attendance in the United States had fallen to about half the levels reported in typical social surveys by the 1990s, the gap between the two having widened steadily over the preceding decades. No similar evidence has yet been provided for Ireland, though anecdotal evidence from parish clergy on actual church attendance levels at weekends would suggest that some degree of over-reporting in social surveys is likely to occur in this country too.

Figure 3 (below) shows the trend in the proportion of adults in Ireland claiming that they attend church at least weekly since 1973. The trend line is almost flat and continues to exceed 80 per cent until the early 1990s. A decline sets in in the early 1990s, and by the end of the decade the level had fallen to 59 per cent for the whole adult population and 63 per cent for self-declared Catholics. How much these levels are inflated at any point in time by over-reporting is impossible to say. However, even if the reported levels are more accurate as an indication of what Irish people think they *ought* to be doing rather than of their actual behaviour, they are still high, despite the decline of recent years, and indicate a cultural valuation of weekly church attendance that is exceptionally strong by international standards.

Figure 3.   **Weekly church attendance in Ireland, 1973-1999**

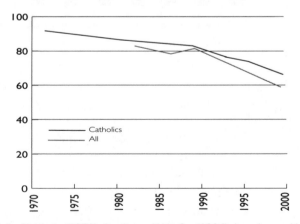

Sources: Nic Ghiolla Phádraig (1976), Breslin and Weafer (1984), Lansdowne Market Research (1994), EVS 1981, 1990, 1999-2000.

Breakdowns of church attendance rates in Ireland by age, social class and rural-urban location show sharply different rates across these social categories (Table 1, below). Weekly attendance has fallen to 27 per cent among young adults (those aged 18-30) and is lowest of all (at 13 per cent) among the urban working class segment of that age-group ('urban' is here defined to refer to population centres of 5,000 or greater). This age-gradient indicates that weekly church attendance has already become a minority practice among young adults, and as this cohort ages low levels of attendance are likely to become generalised through the population. Thus the downward movement in attendance rates shown in Figure 2 shows every likelihood of continuing into the future, and perhaps even intensifying as time passes. Generally speaking, rural-urban and manual-non-manual differences in attendance rates are quite strong up to mid-life, with the rates for the rural non-manual class (which includes farm families) holding up quite well.

To place overall Irish church attendance levels in comparative context, data for European countries on this issue are shown in Figure 4 (p. 53) . This graph is based on the now conventional definition of regular church attendance used in comparative research, which is

Table 1.   **Weekly church attendance by age, social class and rural-urban location in Ireland, 1999-2000**

Social class & rural-urban location	Age group				
	18-30	31-45	46-60	60+	All
Non-manual:					
Rural	61	69	86	94	76
Urban	24	42	73	91	49
Manual:					
Rural	32	63	78	85	63
Urban	13	45	78	82	50
All	27	56	77	89	59

attendance at church at least once per month (weekly church attendance now being so rare in so many countries that comparisons based on that measure are felt to be an overly narrow indicator which would overstate the level of non-participation in church activities). In this comparison, Ireland belongs to a group of only three countries (Malta and Poland being the other two) with monthly church attendance rates comfortably exceeding 70 per cent. Northern Ireland comes close behind at 60 per cent. At the other end of the range, in no society has monthly church attendance disappeared entirely, but in fourteen out of the thirty-three societies it has fallen below 20 per cent. This compares to a total of only eight societies with monthly attendance rates of 50 per cent or higher.

Figure 4.   **Adults who attend church at least monthly**

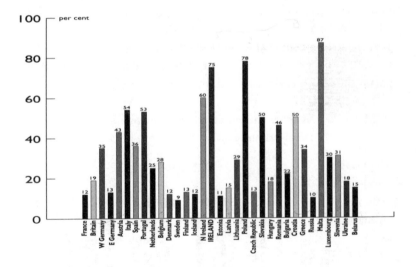

It is also instructive to look at the opposite of regular church attendance – never attending church at all (Figure 5, p. 54). Along with disaffiliation from church membership, this could be considered a key indicator of the abandonment of formal religious practice which secularisation theorists point to. France is the leader in this regard, with 60 per cent claiming that they never attend church, closely followed by Britain, East Germany and the Czech Republic. Sweden, oddly, is at the other extreme with zero per cent who never attend church (Sweden's anomalous position is explained by the widespread Swedish practice of attending church at the major Christian festivals, especially Christmas and Easter, but of staying away from church otherwise). Setting aside the case of Sweden, Ireland is one of only five societies which score below 10 per cent on this indicator (the others being Poland, Romania, Greece and Malta). The fall in weekly church attendance in Ireland in recent years, therefore, arises only to a small degree because of an increase in complete non-attendance and is due much more to a switch from weekly towards less regular attendance. Thus, Irish people are easing off on church attendance rather than abandoning it, in a European context where abandonment has become the majority experience in a small number of countries and the practice of a large minority in many others.

Figure 5.   **Adults who never attend church**

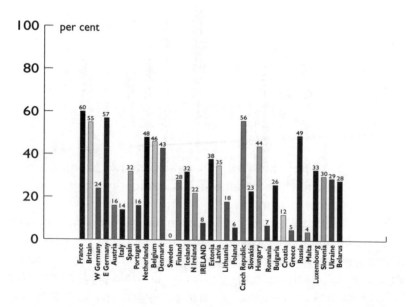

The 1999-2000 EVS included a question about respondents' levels of church attendance when they were twelve years old. This gives us an indication of the extent to which present-day Europeans grew up in non-religious households and are second generation rather than first generation non-attenders at church. It also enables us to establish whether there is any significant movement in the opposite direction *towards* rather than away from regular church attendance, as in the case of those whose church attendance may have risen rather than decreased since they were children.

Figure 6.   **Present-day adults who never attended church when they were around 12 years old**

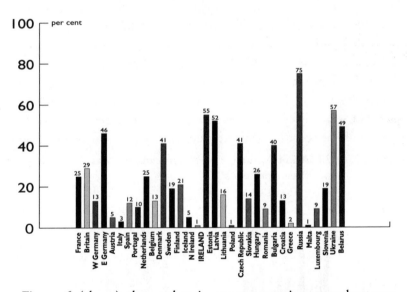

Figure 6 (above) shows that in most countries, complete non-attendance at church in childhood was a minority experience, and Ireland was one of a number of countries where it was virtually unknown. Only in certain former communist countries, especially those within the Soviet Union, did it rise above 50 per cent, with Russia being the extreme case at 75 per cent. Denmark has the highest incidence of complete non-attendance in childhood among the western European countries (41 per cent), but the corresponding incidence among present-day adults, as shown in Figure 5 above, is only slightly higher (43 per cent). Compared to the high levels of complete non-attendance at church among adults in France and Britain shown in Figure 5 above, the childhood levels for these countries are quite low (25 and 29 per cent respectively) indicating that the increase in complete non-attendance at church since childhood has been particularly high in those two countries.

Drawing out these indicators of church attendance somewhat further, Figures 7 (below) and 8 (p. 57) show the percentages of the population in European countries whose church attendance has increased or decreased since childhood. (Decrease in this instance could mean a change from weekly to monthly attendance, from monthly attendance to attendance three or four times a year, or any other decline in level of attendance, while increase could mean any movement in the opposite direction. It is thus more encompassing that movement into or out of the complete non-attendance at church referred to earlier.) These figures show that decrease is by far the more common experience, but there are certain instances of increase. In Ireland, 43 per cent have less frequent church attendance now than in

Figure 7.   **Adults whose church attendance has declined since they were aged 12**

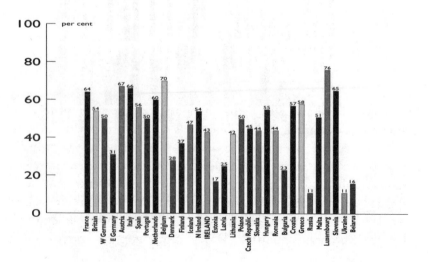

childhood, but 8 per cent report more frequent attendance. Generally speaking, increase in Europe is most likely to have occurred in those countries where levels of attendance were low in childhood – which, on reflection, is as one might expect since these are the countries with the greatest scope for increase. The highest levels of increase are recorded in Belarus, Ukraine, Russia, Estonia and Latvia. However, as we saw in Figure 4 above, these countries were starting from a very low base of attendance and still end up having among the lowest rates of regular church attendance rates in Europe today. Thus, it would be overstating matters to read these figures as indicating a surge towards regular religious attendance in those countries.

Figure 8   **Adults whose church attendance has increased since they were aged 12**

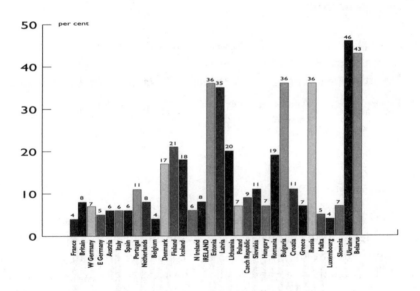

Confidence in Church

The final indicator of people's orientation to churchly religion which we will look at here is their level of confidence in the church as an institution. In Ireland, confidence in the church could be expected to have taken quite a battering during the 1990s, in the aftermath of the succession of clerical scandals which emerged from 1992 onwards.[6] Figures from the three rounds of the EVS surveys in Ireland confirm that a sharp decline in confidence has taken place (Table 2, below). The proportions of adults who have 'a great deal' of confidence in the church was down to 22 per cent in 1999-2000, compared to 40 per cent in 1990 and 51 per cent in 1981. Correspondingly, the proportion with 'not a great deal' of confidence in the church doubled between 1981 and 1999-2000 (from 18 to 37 per cent).

Table 2   **Confidence in Church in Ireland, 1981-1999**

	1981	1990	1999
		Per cent	
A great deal	51	40	22
Quite a lot	27	33	32
Not a great deal	18	24	37
None at all	4	4	9
Total	100	100	100

However, despite the declines of the 1990s, the overall level of confidence in the church was still reasonably high. Just over half the population gave the church a positive confidence rating in 1999-2000 (that is, combining those with a 'great deal' and 'quite a lot' of confidence, which together accounted for 54 per cent of the population). This is a level of public esteem which compares favourably with that of most other major institutions in Irish public life (such as trade unions, the civil service, the press and the armed forces, all of which received much lower confidence ratings than the church). By the end of the 1990s, therefore, the Catholic Church in Ireland may have been brought down off the high pedestal it had occupied in earlier decades.[7] But it still remained one of the most respected institutions in Irish life, and one might be as impressed by its resilience in this regard in the face of adversity as by the extent of its fall from grace.

Self-definition as Religious or Atheistic

We now turn away from indicators of people's orientation towards formal church religion and look instead at the realm of informal or privatised religion. Here the question is to what degree people retain religious orientations that require no allegiance to or participation in a church but can exist as a matter of personal belief or practice.

The first measure of such orientations we look at is given by people's responses to the question, 'Do you think of yourself as a religious person, not a religious person, or a convinced atheist?'. Figure 9 (below) shows that in a large and varied range of countries, both in eastern and western Europe, well over half the population think of themselves as religious. In fourteen out of the thirty-three countries,

Figure 9   Adults who define themselves as religious

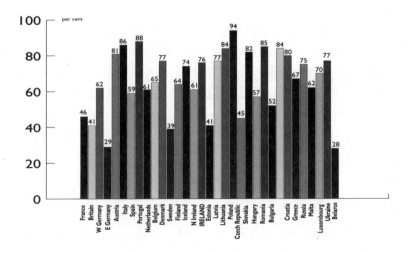

75 per cent of the population or more think of themselves in this way. Ireland's score on this measure, though reasonably high, is far from being the highest – it is exceeded by that of twelve other countries. Thus, although Ireland is one of the leading countries in Europe when it comes to formal religious practice, Irish people are less inclined to consider themselves religious than are the people of many societies where formal practice has dwindled to low levels.

Figure 10   Adults who define themselves as convinced atheist

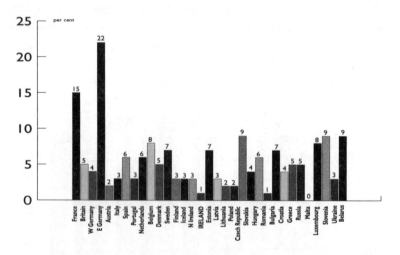

Figure 10 (above) shows the proportions of people who define themselves as the extreme opposite of religious, that is, as atheistic. It is clear from this graph that however indifferent people may be to religion, atheism is not a concept they widely identify with – not even in eastern Europe where atheism had been official communist dogma for so long. East Germany is the only society where more than 20 per cent of the population are willing to refer to themselves as atheist, and France is next highest with 15 per cent. In other countries, including Ireland, self-defined atheists account from small, often tiny, proportions of the population (the figure in Ireland being 1 per cent). Virtually nowhere in Europe, therefore, has secularisation advanced to such an extent that substantial proportions of the population are prepared to assertively embrace atheism. Irish people share in this reluctance, but the degree to which they do so is not at all unusual among European nations.

As the low proportions of atheists in most European countries might lead us to expect, belief in God is widespread and is common even among people who have no connection with any church (Figure 11, below). East Germany and the Czech Republic are the only two societies where less than half the population say they believe in God. Elsewhere, the proportions who claim such belief are high, rising above 80 per cent in 18 of the 33 societies in Figure 11. In Ireland, belief in God is nearly universal, but the same is true of a number of other countries.

Figure 11   **Adults who believe in God**

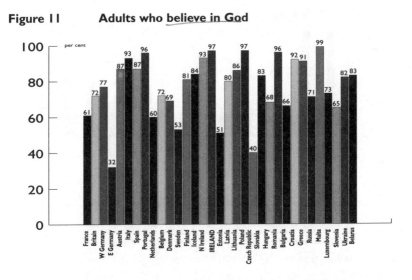

It might be said that belief in God can have little meaning if it is not accompanied by some active relationship with the divine in people's daily lives. One common indication of such a relationship is the practice of prayer, while the absence of prayer might reflect an indifference to the divine that amounts to a *de facto* atheism. Here we look at the second of these two indicators – the proportions of the population in European countries who report that they never pray

(Figure 12, p. 62). These proportions vary widely across countries but are often quite high, thus giving the lie to some extent to the generally widespread belief in God depicted in Figure 11. In eight of the thirty-three societies in Figure 12, over half the population say that they never pray, while in only four societies (Ireland, Poland, Romania and Malta) does the proportion who never pray fall below 10 per cent. This measure of religiosity (or rather of irreligiosity), though relating to a private form of religious orientation, carries loose echoes with the levels of attachment to formal church religion looked at earlier. Broadly speaking, societies where church membership and church attendance have held up reasonably well are also more likely to have held on to a widespread practice of prayer.

Figure 12   Adults who never pray

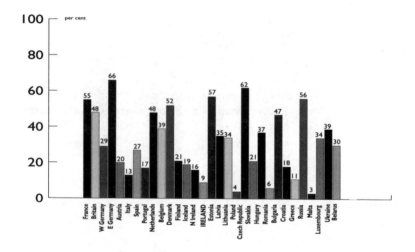

Rites of Passage Religion

Analysis of the role of religion in diverse cultures shows that one of its most basic and widespread functions is to ease people through times of crisis and fundamental change in their lives. This is as true of religion in developed Western societies as anywhere else. Secular symbols and rites have had only limited success in taking over the role of the established religions as providers of rites of passage, the ritual means which help people cope with moments of transition from one condition in life to another. In the Western tradition, three such moments have long been and remain particularly important – birth, marriage and death. As a final means of probing people's orientation to religion, we can look here at responses to the EVS survey question on the whether or not respondents think it important to have religious ceremonies at these moments of transition in life.

The data confirm that the tendency to turn to religion at these moments is still strong, as Table 3 (below) shows. In only three out of the 33 societies in this table (East Germany, the Netherlands and the Czech Republic) does the proportion of the population who consider it important to have religious ceremonies at births, marriages and deaths fall below 50 per cent. Generally speaking, more people are keen to have religious ceremonies on the way out of this world (at death) than on the way in (at birth), but the difference is not great. In Ireland, over 90 per cent of the population think it important to have religious ceremonies at all three kinds of transition event.

Table 3   **Percentage of adults who think it important to have religious ceremonies at births, marriages and deaths**

	Birth	Death	Marriage
		Per cent	
France	61	73	66
Britain	60	80	70
W Germany	73	80	75
E Germany	27	39	34
Austria	82	86	78
Italy	89	89	85
Spain	78	80	75
Portugal	90	92	88
Netherlands	39	55	44
Belgium	67	72	68
Denmark	65	80	63
Sweden	60	77	62
Finland	84	89	82
Iceland	74	91	67

N Ireland	80	91	89
Ireland	**92**	**96**	**93**
Estonia	63	75	65
Latvia	65	88	78
Lithuania	92	95	88
Poland	96	96	95
Czechia	43	51	42
Slovakia	82	85	80
Hungary	76	81	75
Romania	98	98	98
Bulgaria	78	89	83
Croatia	89	94	94
Greece	67	87	83
Russia	76	79	55
Malta	96	97	96
Luxembourg	71	77	67
Slovenia	73	77	70
Ukraine	87	86	70
Belarus	84	88	61

Conclusion

This chapter has looked at indicators of people's orientation both to formal churchly religion and informal or private religion in Ireland and Europe. These indicators have shown that extensive detachment from churchly religion is the dominant position in many European countries, particularly in a number of former communist countries but also in certain western European societies. Even in these countries, detachment is nowhere universal, in that no country is lacking at least a small minority with continuing regular participation in church activities. On the other side of the balance sheet, there are many European countries where church participation remains quite high, both in the east and in the west. Ireland, like Poland in the east, is one of these. Declines in participation have occurred in Ireland in recent years, and the age-profile of formal religious practice suggest that it will continue to decline further as the present young-adult population ages. Confidence in the church has also declined over the years, especially since the advent of church scandals in the 1990s. However, few Irish people go so far as to detach themselves totally from the church. The vast majority still identify themselves as church members, and three-quarters claim to go to church at least monthly. It is quite possible that people overstate the frequency of their church attendance, but even if they do, that very fact is an indication how many Irish people think they *ought* to be going to church regularly. As such, it reflects a positive valuation of formal religious practice which shows remarkable durability and which is well in excess of that found in many other countries.

Though there are fewer devout people in Ireland than there were in the past, there has been little by way of a corresponding increase in the numbers of atheists, or whatever one might call those who reject religion outright. Despite the scaling down of formal religious practice, the vast majority of people continue to believe in God, to consider themselves religious, and to think it important to have religious ceremonies at births, marriages and deaths. They are reluctant to refer to themselves as atheists or to declare that they never pray. Most European populations are similar to Irish people as far as these informal aspects of religiosity are concerned. Some countries with low levels of formal religious practice are somewhat weaker in these respects than others, but generally the persistence and prevalence of these religious orientations is the more striking. It is difficult to know how deeply these orientations impinge on people's daily lives, or whether they are profound enough to merit being labelled as religious in any serious sense of that term. Nevertheless, they are there. They give comfort to those who would argue that religion is likely always to be with us, and that out and out secularisation is a figment of the social scientific imagination that is unlikely ever to be universally realised, either in Ireland or in any other part of the world.

Notes
1. See Sherkat and Ellison 1999; Bruce 1999.
2. See Stark and Finke 2000.
3. See Stark and Finke 2000, 73-74; Need and Evans 2001.
4. See Fogarty *et al* 1984 and Whelan 1994 for reports on the Irish data from these earlier surveys.

5.   See Sherkat and Ellison 1999.
6.   See Kenny 1997; Inglis 1998.
7.   This is revealed, for example, by Biever's survey of Dublin Catholics in
     1962 – see Biever 1976.

References

Biever, B.F. *Religion, Culture, and Values. A Cross-Cultural Analysis of Motivational Factors in Native Irish and American Irish Catholicism*, New York, Arno Press, 1976.

Breslin, A. and Weafer. J. *Religious Beliefs, Practices and Moral Attitudes. A Comparison of Two Irish Surveys, 1974-1984*, Report No. 21, Maynooth, Council for Research and Development, 1985.

Bruce, S. *Choice & Religion: A Critique of Rational Choice*, Oxford, Oxford University Press, 1999.

Fogarty, M., L. Ryan and J. Lee, *Irish Values and Attitudes. The Irish Report of the European Values Study System*, Dublin, Dominican Publications, 1984.

Hayes, B. 'Religious independents within western industrialised nations: A socio-demographic profile', *Sociology of Religion* 61:2 (2000), pp. 191-207.

Inglis, T. *Moral Monopoly. The Rise and Fall of the Catholic Church in Ireland*, Dublin, University College Dublin Press, 1998.

Kenny, M. *Goodbye to Catholic Ireland*, London, Sinclair-Stevenson, 1997.

Lansdowne Market Research. *Mass Attendance, Omnibus Survey, March 1994*, Dublin, Lansdowne Market Research, 1994.

Sherkat, D.E. and C. G. Ellison, 'Recent developments and current controversies in the sociology of religion', *Annual Review of Sociology* 25 (1999), pp. 363-394.

Need, A. and G. Evans, 'Analysing patterns of religious participation in post-communist Eastern Europe', *The British Journal of Sociology* 52:2 (2001), pp. 229-248.

Nic Ghiolla Phádraig, M. 'Religion in Ireland' *Social Studies*, 5 (1976), pp. 113-180.

Stark, R. and R. Finke, *Acts of Faith. Explaining the human side of religion*, Berkeley, University of California Press, 2000.

Presser, S. and L. Stinson, 'Data collection mode and social desirability bias in self-reported religious attendance', *American Sociological Review*, 6:1 (1998), pp. 137-145 Whelan, C.T. (ed.), *Values and Social Change in Ireland*, Dublin, Gill & Macmillan, 1994.

Intimations of Immorality: An Analysis of the ISSP 1998

CONOR K. WARD

When Pope John Paul II wrote his 1982 letter founding the Pontifical Council for Culture he used a very sociological description of culture as 'the ethos of a people'. It is culture in the sense of shared beliefs, shared patterns of behaviour, shared attitudes. This article discusses the extent to which the ethos of the people of the Republic of Ireland is religious. It is based on information provided by those interviewed when the International Social Survey Programme (ISSP) chose religion as the theme for its research in 1998. Ethos is not bounded by territorial limits, so data relating to Ireland is set in the context of data from the other member countries of the ISSP. Differences by age groups are also examined. On central religious beliefs, the Irish ISSP survey data appear to indicate considerable consensus. A belief in a God was reported by over 9 in 10; in Heaven by over 8 in 10; in Life after Death by just under 8 in 10. Belief in Hell was lower at about half. Almost three quarters of adults said that they attend church 2 or 3 times a month or more often and the percentage of 18-28 year olds was 47 per cent. Confidence in churches and religious organisations declined steadily from the oldest at 59 per cent to 7 per cent of the 18-28 year olds, but 57 per cent of 18-28 year olds had confidence in their local priest. On moral matters autonomy of judgement rather than acceptance of authority was general and almost total among 18-28 year olds.

Introduction

When Pope John Paul II wrote his 1982 letter founding the Pontifical Council for Culture he used a very sociological description of culture as 'the ethos of a people'. It is culture in the sense of shared beliefs, shared patterns of behaviour, shared attitudes. It reflects the derivation of the word culture as what is revered.

This article is based on information provided by those interviewed when the International Social Survey Programme (ISSP) chose religion as the theme for its research in 1998 and some thoughts for discussion are suggested. Ethos is not bounded by territorial limits, so data relating to Ireland is set in the context of data from the other member countries of the ISSP. Differences by age groups are also examined. The ISSP insists on having the same standardised questions asked in each country with the objective of making international comparisons possible in its 38 member countries. International information is taken from the 32 sets of data currently available – for Ireland and 28 countries, and former West Germany, former East Germany and Northern Ireland with their separate data sets. (In the text the Republic of Ireland and the Republic of the Philippines have been abbreviated to Ireland and the Philippines, respectively.) Those interviewed in each area were a probability sample of at least 1000 adults. In Ireland 1010 were interviewed in May-June 1998, using the Voters Register as a sampling frame. Further information about methodology is provided in an Appendix.

Patterns of Religious Beliefs

Beliefs are central to the ethos of a people and, fortunately, the ISSP Survey provides a lot of data on beliefs, and also on attitudes, and a limited amount on behaviour. On central religious beliefs, the Irish ISSP survey data appear to indicate considerable consensus. A belief in a God was reported by over 9 in 10; in Heaven over 8 in 10; in life after death just under 8 in 10. Belief in Hell was lower at about half. You can see why Wordsworth's ode 'Intimations of Immortality' came back to me from distant schooldays as a title for this article. The final words of the Ode are 'Let us sing of somewhat higher things ...'

Belief in God in Ireland

Belief in a God is central to a discussion of the extent to which the ethos of the Irish is religious. It is therefore given special attention with, first, detailed data for Ireland and then an international context with data from the 32 ISSP surveys available in June 2000.

What kind of belief was the belief in God? A request to indicate what best described their belief in God within a choice of four responses produced the following pattern in Ireland: 'I don't believe in God now and I never have' (1 per cent); 'I don't believe in God now, but I used to' (6 per cent); 'I believe in God now, but I didn't used to' (5 per cent); 'I believe in God now and I always have' (89 per cent).

Another question asked which of six statements 'comes closest to expressing what you believe about God'. In the order in which the statements appeared, the results were: 'I don't believe in God' (2 per cent); 'I don't know whether there is a God and I don't think that there is any way to find out' (4 per cent); I don't believe in a personal God, but I do believe in a higher power of some kind' (7 per cent); I find myself believing in God some of the time, but not at others' (9 per cent); 'While I have doubts, I feel that I do believe in God' (28 per cent); ' I know God really exists and I have no doubts about it' (50 per cent). No one chose the option 'Can't choose, don't know'.

There was also a question 'Do you agree or disagree with the following – There is a God who concerns himself with every human being personally?' In Ireland those who agreed were 78 per cent of the respondents, those who disagreed were 10 per cent, those who said they neither agreed nor disagreed were 7 per cent. 'Can't choose, don't know' was the response of 3 per cent.

Looking separately at age groups, the percentage 'believing in God now' declines gradually by 1 per cent each ten years approximately from 99 per cent of the oldest (who were 69 and over) to those aged 29-38 at 93 per cent and then falls sharply to 84 per cent for the youngest, who were the 18-28 year olds in the sample. The percentage whose belief was in a Higher Power rather than a personal God rose gradually from 2 per cent of those 69 and over to 8 per cent of 29-38 year olds and 14 per cent of the 18-28 year olds.

The ISSP questions and their wording are decided at an AGM of the ISSP members and all the questions must be asked in each country exactly as worded, so that comparisons can be made, but there are also optional questions which are asked at the end in some countries. In Ireland and some other countries that facility was used to try to ascertain the image people have of the God in whom they believe. So we have additional information for Ireland for four separate scales of contrasting images of God. Those interviewed were asked to indicate how they would place themselves on a scale of 1 to 7 for four sets of contrasting images of God. Three per cent did not answer the question. Eighty per cent said that their image of God was as Friend equally with or more than King, 39 per cent had an image of God as Mother equally with or more than Father, 43 per cent had an image of God as Spouse equally with or more than Master, 4 per cent had an image of God as Lover equally with or more than Judge.

The pattern of images of God by age groups was complicated. The percentage who said that their image of God was as Friend equally or more than King was similar for all age groups at 80 per cent. The percentage who said that their image of God was as Mother equally or more than Father rose with decreasing age from 22 per cent of those aged 69 and over to 32 per cent of those aged 59-68 and 38 per cent of those aged 49-58. The age groups below the 49 year olds were all similar at 46 per cent. The percentage who said that their image of God was as Spouse equally or more than Master was lowest for those aged 59-68 and 69 and over at 31 per cent. Next lowest were those aged 18-28 at 40 per cent and those aged 49-58 at 44 per cent. The percentage for those aged 29-38 was 51 per cent and that for 39-48 was 55 per cent. The percentage who said that their image of God was as Lover equally or more than Judge was lowest for those aged 69 and over at 38 per cent and next lowest were those aged 59-68 and those aged 18-28 at 47 per cent. The percentage for those aged 49-58 was

51 per cent and that for those aged 39-48 was 56 per cent. The highest were those aged 29-38 at 67 per cent.

Beliefs in God – the international context
The paragraphs which follow will present data from the 32 surveys currently available. Since Ireland is the central focus of this paper, Ireland (for the abbreviated Republic of Ireland) and Northern Ireland are highlighted in each section.

Belief in a God was highest in Chile (96 per cent), Cyprus (96 per cent), Poland (95 per cent), the Philippines (95 per cent), and **Ireland** (94 per cent). Results elsewhere, in descending order, were: USA, Portugal and **Northern Ireland** (from 92 per cent to 90 per cent); Italy, Israel, Spain and Austria (from 89 per cent to 80 per cent); Canada, Switzerland, Slovakia and Latvia (from 79 per cent to 70 per cent); New Zealand, Australia, Great Britain, Former West Germany, Hungary, Slovenia and Bulgaria (from 69 per cent to 60 per cent); Norway, the Netherlands, Denmark, Sweden, France and Russia (from 59 per cent to 50 per cent), the Czech Republic (46 per cent); Japan (43 per cent); and former East Germany (25 per cent).

Belief in a God who is concerned with every human being personally was over 80 per cent only in The Philippines, where it was 88 per cent. Results elsewhere, in descending order, were: **Ireland**, Chile, Poland, Portugal, USA and Cyprus (from 79 per cent to 70 per cent); **Northern Ireland** (66 per cent); Israel (64 per cent); Italy and Slovakia (54 per cent); Canada, Latvia, Spain, New Zealand and Switzerland (from 49 per cent to 40 per cent); Australia, Denmark, Russia, Austria, Bulgaria, Britain, Former West Germany, Norway, the Netherlands and Hungary (from 39 per cent to 30 per cent); France, Japan, Slovenia, Sweden and Czech Republic (from 29 per cent to 20 per cent). The percentage in former East Germany was 15 per cent.

Images of God was an optional question in the ISSP survey and was asked in a small number of countries in whole or in part. An image of God as Mother equally or more than Father had the following pattern: Hungary (55 per cent), Australia (51 per cent), Canada (49 per cent), Latvia (47 per cent), Slovakia (44 per cent),

France (43 per cent), New Zealand (41 per cent), **Ireland** (39 per cent), Switzerland (36 per cent), and USA (33 per cent). An image of God as Spouse equally or more than Master had the following pattern: Czech Republic (70 per cent), Australia (54 per cent), Latvia (51 per cent), Canada (51 per cent), France (50 per cent), New Zealand (45 per cent), **Ireland** (43 per cent), Slovakia (40 per cent), Hungary (35 per cent), and USA (33 per cent). An image of God as Lover equally or more than Judge had the following pattern: Czech Republic (91 per cent), Portugal (88 per cent), France (81 per cent), Slovakia (78 per cent), Canada (56 per cent), New Zealand (52 per cent), Australia (52 per cent), Hungary (51 per cent), **Ireland** (49 per cent), and Latvia (44 per cent). An image of God as Friend equally with or more than King had the following pattern: **Ireland** (80 per cent), Australia (77 per cent), New Zealand (76 per cent), Canada (76 per cent), Hungary (69 per cent), and USA (66 per cent).

Other Central Religious Beliefs

Life after death
Belief in life after death, definitely and probably, was highest in the Philippines (87 per cent), USA (81 per cent) and Cyprus (80 per cent). Below 80 per cent belief in life after death, definitely and probably, had the following pattern in descending order: Poland, **Ireland**, Chile, **Northern Ireland**, Portugal, Italy and Switzerland (from 79 per cent to 70 per cent); Slovakia, Israel, New Zealand and Austria (from 69 per cent to 60 per cent); the Netherlands, Great Britain, Canada, Spain, former West Germany, Norway, Latvia, Japan, Australia, Sweden and France (from 59 per cent to 50 per cent); Czech Republic, Slovenia, Denmark and Russia (from 44 per cent to 40 per cent); Hungary (39 per cent), Bulgaria (34 per cent), and Former East Germany (15 per cent).

Religious miracles
Belief in religious miracles was highest in Cyprus at 89 per cent. Chile was 81 per cent and Portugal and the United States were 79 per cent.

Below 79 per cent belief in religious miracles, definitely and probably, had the following pattern in descending order: The Philippines (76 per cent), Italy (72 per cent), and **Ireland** (71 per cent); Poland, Austria, Former West Germany, Israel and Switzerland (from 69 per cent to 60 per cent); **Northern Ireland**, Slovenia, Canada and Slovakia (from 59 per cent to 50 per cent); New Zealand, Spain and the Netherlands (from 46 per cent to 40 per cent); Norway, Great Britain, former East Germany, France, Australia, Russia, Latvia, Czech Republic and Hungary (from 39 per cent to 30 per cent); Bulgaria, Japan, Sweden and Denmark (from 29 per cent to 25 per cent).

Heaven and Hell

Belief in Heaven and Belief in Hell varied very considerably and not consistently. The most interesting way to present the pattern of beliefs appears to be to provide information for the two side by side, in descending order of belief in Heaven.

	Belief in Heaven	Belief in Hell
The Philippines	96	88
USA	86	74
IRELAND	**84**	**53**
NORTHERN IRELAND	**83**	**71**
Chile	82	59
Poland	78	68
Cyprus	77	76
Portugal	76	64
Italy	68	59
Canada	63	47
New Zealand	58	37
Slovakia	57	49
Great Britain	53	32
Switzerland	53	30
Spain	51	37
Israel	51	58
The Netherlands	47	26
Australia	47	40
Former West Germany	46	46
Austria	45	31

Japan	44	37
Norway	41	19
Hungary	36	28
Slovenia	35	36
Latvia	33	31
France	33	20
Denmark	32	16
Russia	31	31
Czech Republic	29	23
Sweden	28	14
Bulgaria	27	25
Former East Germany	22	11

Patterns of other beliefs

As already mentioned, the ISSP protocols provide for a small number of questions described as 'Optional'. In the 1998 ISSP survey on religion there were questions about other beliefs. There were, in sequence, four statements with a choice of five answers to each: Definitely true, Probably true, Probably false, Definitely false, Can't choose.

That 'Good luck charms sometimes do bring good luck' was described as definitely or probably true in the following pattern: the highest, at 72 per cent, was Bulgaria, Russia was 57 per cent and the Czech Republic was 50 per cent. The other available data were, in descending order: Slovakia, former West Germany, Portugal and Switzerland (from 49 per cent to 40 per cent); the Philippines, Austria, former East Germany, Hungary and New Zealand (from 35 per cent to 33 per cent); Canada (29 per cent), **Ireland** (25 per cent), France (24 per cent), and the Netherlands (21 per cent).

That 'Some fortune tellers really can foresee the future' was described as definitely or probably true in the following pattern: The highest were Latvia (80 per cent), Czech Republic (71 per cent), Slovakia and Russia (68 per cent), and Bulgaria (65 per cent). The other available data were, in descending order: New Zealand, Hungary and Switzerland (from 46 per cent to 40 per cent); France, Canada, the Philippines, former West Germany and Austria (from 39 per cent to 30 per cent); **Ireland**, the Netherlands and Portugal (28 per cent); former East Germany (21 per cent).

That 'Some faithhealers do have God-given healing powers' was described as definitely or probably true in the following pattern: The highest were Latvia (81 per cent), **Ireland** (75 per cent) and Slovakia (71 per cent). The other available data were, in descending order: Bulgaria, Russia and Czech Republic (from 65 per cent to 62 per cent); The Philippines (54 per cent); Switzerland, Austria, New Zealand and Former West Germany (from 48 per cent to 43 per cent); France, Portugal, Canada and Former East Germany (from 38 per cent to 33 per cent); The Netherlands (28 per cent).

That 'A persons star sign at birth, or horoscope, can affect the course of their future' was described as definitely or probably true in the following pattern: The highest were Latvia (66 per cent), Bulgaria (65 per cent) and former East Germany (63 per cent). The other available data were, in descending order: Russia (56 per cent), Czech Republic (54 per cent); Slovakia, Switzerland, former West Germany, France and Hungary (from 49 per cent to 40 per cent); Austria, New Zealand, the Philippines and Portugal (from 36 per cent to 30 per cent), the Netherlands (24 per cent), Canada (23 per cent), and **Ireland** (19 per cent).

Some thoughts for discussion

After each section of survey data thoughts for discussion are inserted – some reflections from the author and some quotations from others.

There is a difference between atheism and agnosticism that should be kept in mind. Looking at the ISSP data one finds that adding the percentage believing in God and the percentage who say they are atheist they always add to less than 100 per cent. The gap increases as the percentage believing in God decreases – when about 70 per cent believe in God there was a gap of 20 per cent and when about 50 per cent believed in God the gap was around 30 per cent. An exception to the trend was the area with the lowest percentage believing in God, fFormer East Germany, where 25 per cent said that they believed in God and 51 per cent said that they were Atheists, leaving a gap of only 24 per cent.

Theologian Dermot Lane wrote: 'Beliefs must be seen to be related to, and saying something about, human experience without however being reduced simply to the level of human experience'.[1] According to sociologist Tony Fahey: 'Recent scholarship, however, challenges the conventional wisdom in this area and has queried virtually every aspect of the general thesis that socio-economic development and secularisation go hand in hand. … Taking its line from neo-classical economics this approach argues that an underlying interest in religion – that is, a "demand" for religion among the general public – is much closer to being a constant than is usually assumed, though the precise focus of that demand may vary. The factors which change more fundamentally, and which account for the changing fortunes of organised religion, lie rather on the supply side, that is, in the way religious organisations (churches) gain or lose the capability to track and respond to popular demand for religion'.[2]

Patterns of Religious Behaviour
Behaviour has fewer questions in the ISSP Survey than beliefs and attitudes. There are questions on church attendance/attendance at religious Services, prayer and indicating 'No religion'.

Patterns in Ireland: stated attendance at religious services in Ireland
Attendance at religious services was the main item of religious behaviour included in the ISSP survey. The question was worded 'How often do you currently attend religious services?' (with variations in some countries, mentioned later). The index very frequently used is attendance once a week or more often, which is also the official appropriate attendance according to the Church of 95 per cent of the Irish respondents in the survey. From the perspective of interest in shared behaviour as an element of the ethos of a society, attendance two or three times a month or more often may be a relevant indicator. Both are available in the ISSP scale of answers, along with less frequent attendance.

In Ireland the stated attendance 'once a week, nearly every week' was 63 per cent, '2 or 3 times a month' or more often was 73 per cent and once a month or more often was 78 per cent. Attendance 'several times a year' was the response of 12 per cent. 'Less than once a year' was the response of 6 per cent and that of 5 per cent was 'never'. From a perspective of interest in shared ethos that means that almost three quarters of adults said that they attend church two or three times a month or more often. Stated attendance several times a year or more often came to 90 per cent.

The pattern of stated weekly attendance by age group was a steady decline from nine tenths of those aged 69 to a third of those aged 18-28. Among 18-28 year olds 47 per cent said that they attended two or three times a month or more often, once a month was the stated attendance of 6 per cent, several times a year was that of 23 per cent, less frequently than once a year was the reply of 17 per cent and never was that of 7 per cent.

Church attendance is part of the standard demographic information collected in every ISSP survey at the end of the interview. Looking at stated church attendance over a ten-year period it emerges that in Ireland the percentage who say that they attend two or three times a month or more often is lower than in other years in 1991 and 1998, the two years in which the subject of the survey was religion.

Prayer

In reply to a question 'Thinking now about the present, about how often do you pray' 45 per cent of the Irish respondents said that they prayed at least several times a week and a further 25 per cent every week. (Unfortunately we have no information about everyday prayer.) For several times a month or more the percentage was 84 per cent. Several times a year was 5 per cent, about once or twice a year was 3 per cent, less than once a year was 2 per cent and never was 5 per cent.

No religion

In Ireland those who said they had 'No Religion' were 6 per cent of those interviewed. The percentage increased gradually with decrease in age and reached 12 per cent with the 18 – 28 year olds.

International patterns: stated attendance at religious services

In the ISSP surveys attendance at religious services is information collected in all surveys as part of the demographic data. Unfortunately, being in that section and not among the standardised questions, there was some variation in the categories used in some countries.

The pattern for stated attendance of two or three times a month or more often was as follows: stated attendance at religious services was highest in **Ireland** at 73 per cent, followed by Switzerland at 64 per cent, Poland at 62 per cent and **Northern Ireland** at 51 per cent. The other available data were, in descending order: Italy, Slovakia and Portugal (from 44 per cent to 41 per cent); USA, Chile, Spain and Austria (from 39 per cent to 33 per cent); Canada (29 per cent); Slovenia, New Zealand, Australia, Hungary and the Netherlands (from 23 per cent to 18 per cent). It was 17 per cent in former West Germany and 16 per cent in former East Germany (very similar, even though they were so different in religious beliefs), and 16 per cent in France. It was 12 per cent in Latvia and the Czech Republic, and below 10 per cent in the other countries for which comparable information was available: Norway, Cyprus, Denmark, Sweden, Russia, and Japan. Great Britain asked 'apart from such special occasions as weddings, funerals and baptism how often nowadays do you attend services or meetings connected with your religion?', which suggests that the stated attendance of 17 per cent two or three times a month or more is not comparable with the other figures given. In the Philippines the question asked was about how often respondents prayed and there were no data from Bulgaria and Israel.

Prayer

In relation to religious ethos two possible indices are prayer 'at least several times a week' and prayer 'never'. The pattern of prayer several times a week or more often was: The highest percentage was in the Philippines, where it was 80 per cent, and next highest were USA (60 per cent), Poland (57 per cent), and Chile (55 per cent). Then in descending order from 47 per cent were: Portugal, **Northern Ireland**,

Ireland and Italy (from 47 per cent to 45 per cent); Slovakia, Hungary, Switzerland, Austria, Australia, The Netherlands and Canada (from 36 per cent to 30 per cent); Spain, Cyprus, New Zealand, Japan, Israel, and former West Germany (from 29 per cent to 25 per cent); Great Britain, France, Latvia and Slovenia (21 per cent); Norway, Czech Republic, Denmark, Russia, Bulgaria and Sweden (from 20 per cent to 16 per cent); former East Germany (8 per cent). The percentage who said that they never prayed was lowest in the Philippines (0 per cent), followed by **Ireland** (5 per cent) and Poland (6 per cent). In ascending order, the percentages above 6 per cent were: Cyprus, USA, Japan, Chile, Portugal, Italy, Switzerland and **Northern Ireland** (from 11 per cent to 17 per cent); Austria, Canada and Slovakia (from 20 per cent to 25 per cent); Spain, former West Germany, Hungary, Great Britain, New Zealand, Latvia, Australia, Slovenia, Norway, Israel and Bulgaria (from 29 per cent to 39 per cent); the Netherlands, France and Sweden (from 42 per cent to 46 per cent); Czech Republic, Denmark and Russia (from 54 per cent to 58 per cent). Former East Germany had the highest percentage saying that they never prayed (70 per cent).

No religion
The international pattern was that indicating that they had no religion was highest in former East Germany (69 per cent), Japan (62 per cent) and the Netherlands (58 per cent). Then the pattern was, in descending order: France (47 per cent), Great Britain (46 per cent), Czech Republic (45 per cent), Latvia (36 per cent), Russia (35 per cent), Canada (31 per cent), New Zealand and Sweden (29 per cent); Australia and Hungary (27 per cent), Slovenia (24 per cent); Slovakia and former West Germany (16 per cent); Spain and USA (14 per cent); Bulgaria (13 per cent); Denmark and Austria (12 per cent); Norway and **Northern Ireland** (10 per cent); Switzerland (9 per cent), Portugal and Italy (8 per cent), Poland and **Ireland** (6 per cent); Chile (5 per cent); and the Philippines (0 per cent). There was no data for Cyprus and Israel.

Some thoughts for discussion

Infrequent attendance at church services may not be regarded as sufficient for the growth of a person's relationship with God as a member of a community of faith, but it might be worth discussing if it is sufficient to maintain an ethos which might be described as religious? It can be suggested that stated and actual attendance may differ. Can it be suggested that, when the focus is a religious ethos, stated attendance is important, even if it may be higher than actual attendance? Another thought – perhaps being regular and inflexible in any pattern of behaviour is something alien to contemporary youth culture? And the index of not attending weekly may not be as significant as once it was?

Sociologist Kieran Flanagan, in a massive book on the subject of how the theologians have misunderstood and misused sociology, defies summary, but I think one can say that he blames a decline in attendance on the elimination of mystery.[3]

According to Psychiatrist Patricia Casey: 'In the U.S. those who attend church frequently are four times less likely to die by suicide than those who never attend … A study published recently in *Psychological Medicine*, the most prestigious psychiatric journal in Europe, found that for men the suicide rates of 19 European countries as well as Canada and the US were linked to religious belief and religious environment.'[4]

Patterns of Attitudes: Confidence in Churches and Religious Organisations

Confidence in churches and religious organisations in Ireland

One ISSP series of questions designed to ascertain attitudes was on confidence in a number of national bodies. The question asked successively 'How much confidence do you have in the Dáil, business and industry, churches and religious organisations, courts and the legal system, schools and the educational system?' and the choice of answers was 'complete confidence', 'a great deal of confidence', 'some confidence', 'very little confidence', 'no confidence at all' and 'can't choose'. In Ireland the pattern of replies of complete confidence and a great deal of confidence taken together was the Dáil (17.4 per cent), business and industry (28 per cent), churches and religious organisations (28 per cent), courts and the legal system (33 per cent), and schools and the educational system (61 per cent).

In regard to the churches and religious organisations the pattern of replies in Ireland was 'Complete confidence' (8 per cent), 'A great deal of confidence' (20 per cent), 'Some confidence' (43 per cent), 'Very little confidence' (18 per cent), 'No confidence at all' (11 per cent). By age groups 'Complete confidence' or 'A great deal of confidence' declined steadily from 59 per cent of those aged over 69 to 7 per cent of those aged 18-28. Those aged 68-59 were relatively similar to those aged 69 and over, at 52 per cent. Then there was a noticeable change to 24 per cent of those aged 58-49, 20 per cent of those aged 48-39, and 21 per cent of those aged 38-29. Those aged 28-18 were very much the lowest at 7 per cent.

In Ireland the facility to include a few extra questions with the ISSP Survey was used to explore confidence in the local representatives of national organisations. The low ratings of the national bodies did not change significantly, with the exception of local priests/clergy, where 42 per cent said that they had complete or a great deal of confidence compared to 28 per cent with that level of confidence in churches and religious organisations. The local Gardaí (police) were those used to correspond to the courts and legal system and complete or a great deal of confidence was expressed in them by 54 per cent compared to 33 per cent for the courts and legal system.

The results for 18-28 year olds regarding local priests/clergy were the most striking comparative percentages, with complete or a great deal of confidence indicated by 57 per cent of this age group compared to 7 per cent with complete or a great deal of confidence in churches and religious organisations. The 18-28 year olds indicated a similar level of confidence in local priests/clergy, local Gardaí and local teachers.

Confidence in churches and religious organisations internationally
Complete or a great deal of confidence was highest in the Philippines
at 72 per cent followed by Chile at 54 per cent. The pattern then was,
in descending order: Cyprus, USA, Portugal, Slovakia, Hungary and
Poland (from 44 per cent to 40 per cent); Russia, Latvia, Spain,
Denmark, **Northern Ireland**, Italy, Australia and Norway (from 39 per
cent to 31 per cent); Israel, **Ireland**, Canada, Austria, former West
Germany, Switzerland, Slovenia, the Netherlands, Bulgaria, New
Zealand and Sweden (from 28 per cent to 21 per cent); Great Britain,
former East Germany, Czech Republic and France (from 17 per cent
to 13 per cent). Japan was 5 per cent.

Some thoughts for discussion
President Mary McAleese:

> Disappointment and impatience in themselves are perhaps no
> bad thing. They are are the vital signs of a people who care. As
> a source of energy they hold the promise of more pressure, more
> change. Left to fester though, they generate a much worse
> enemy – indifference. And as Edmund Burke has remarked
> 'Nothing is so fatal to religion as indifference.[5]

Bishop Donal Murray, in a paper to the Fís conference in April 2000,
having wondered if a creature called 'the institutional Church … is
meant to be another name for the bishops, or, if not, who or what is
meant to be this creature and where is its lair', later said:

> One of the most fundamental challenges for society and for the
> Church today is to relate with individual people in such a way
> as to show them that they actually count, that they do matter.
> This means relating to them in a way that speaks to 'what is
> most deeply human'. The Catch-22 is that if society and the
> Church are seen as soulless institutional structures, they are
> regarded as being, 'by definition' incapable of relating in such a

way. They are not seen as capable of touching those seething depths of restlessness and creativity. Meeting this challenge requires reaching upwards and downwards. The institutions have to find ways of reaching individual people; each person has to find ways of reaching out beyond his or her individual and family concerns to the wider society.[6]

Theologian Liam Walsh, OP, commenting on the results of the ISSP Survey, wrote:

> The survey did not ask Irish people *why* they have the degree of confidence they do have in their local priests, and *why* they do not have a comparable degree of confidence in their bishops. The theologian can have a hypothesis, based on the kind of theology he espouses, which he would invite sociology to test. One such hypothesis, based on a Vatican II type ecclesiology, is that the difference in confidence is related to the different experiences people have of being listened to. A Church in which the *sensus fidelium* means something has to be a Church in which there is a great deal of listening. Priests might be better at listening than bishops.[7]

David Touhy and Penny Cairns, reporting on a study of young adults, said:

> They were highly critical of the values that were being imposed on them and they were even more critical of the manner of imposition ... A consistent theme across the different worlds we explored was a suspicion of authoritarian certainties. Young people put great value on personal experience. The opportunity for participation attracted young people to many different types of activities and their initiation and deeper integration into the world of religion will require strategies that promote participation.[8]

Attitudes about Sexual Relations

Attitudes in Ireland about sexual relations

A series of ISSP questions related to attitudes about sexual relations. The results in Ireland indicate very considerable disagreement with the traditional Christian ethic in this sphere. A man and a woman to have sexual relations before marriage was regarded as always wrong by 30 per cent, almost always wrong by 15 per cent, wrong only sometimes by 16 per cent and not wrong at all by 39 per cent. A married person to have sexual relations with someone other than a spouse was regarded as always wrong by 63 per cent, almost always wrong by 20 per cent, wrong only sometimes by 10 per cent and not wrong at all by 6 per cent. Two adults of the same sex to have sexual relations was regarded as always wrong by 60 per cent, as almost always wrong by 12 per cent, as wrong only sometimes by 10 per cent and as not wrong at all by 18 per cent.

In each case the percentage saying 'always wrong' declined steadily from about 90 per cent of those aged 69 and over to the following percentages for 18-28 year olds: for premarital relations (8 per cent), for extra marital relations (43 per cent) and for same sex relations (30 per cent).

International attitudes about sexual relations

The pattern of the attitude that it is always wrong for a man and a woman to have sexual relations before marriage was: the Philippines (65 per cent), then, in descending order: Chile, Israel, USA and **Ireland** (from 2 per cent to 30 per cent); Bulgaria, **Northern Ireland** and Portugal (from 28 per cent to 23 per cent); Cyprus, Poland, Italy, New Zealand, Hungary, Slovakia, Spain, Russia, Australia, Canada, Japan and Great Britain (from 18 per cent to 12 per cent); Latvia, the Netherlands, Norway, former West Germany, Denmark, Switzerland, France, Sweden, Czech Republic, Austria, Slovenia and Former East Germany (from 9 per cent to 3 per cent).

The pattern of the attitude that it is always wrong for a married man or woman to have sexual relations with someone other than the spouse was: The Philippines (85 per cent), USA (80 per cent). Then, in descending order: Chile, Portugal, Israel, **Northern Ireland** and Poland (from 79 per cent to 70 per cent); Canada, Spain, New Zealand, **Ireland**, Australia, and Denmark (from 69 per cent to 63 per cent); Italy, Sweden, Great Britain, Norway, The Netherlands, Slovakia, Hungary, Cyprus, Slovenia and Bulgaria (from 58 per cent to 50 per cent); Japan, former East Germany, Austria, former West Germany, Switzerland, Latvia and Czech Republic (from 46 per cent to 40 per cent); France (38 per cent), and Russia (34 per cent).

The pattern of the attitude that it is always wrong for two adults of the same sex to have sexual relations was: Chile (88 per cent), the Philippines (85 per cent). Then, in descending order: Poland and Portugal (74 per cent); Bulgaria, **Northern Ireland**, Hungary, USA, Bulgaria and Latvia (from 70 per cent to 61 per cent); **Ireland**, Israel, Cyprus, Slovakia, Italy, New Zealand, Slovenia and Australia (from 60 per cent to 48 per cent); Great Britain, Japan and Canada (from 44 per cent to 40 per cent); France, Norway, former East Germany, Sweden, Austria, Spain, Czech Republic and Denmark (from 38 per cent to 30 per cent); former West Germany (29 per cent), Switzerland (26 per cent), and the Netherlands (16 per cent).

Some thoughts for discussion
Below are some quotes from commentators on the preliminary report on the ISSP data in a special edition of *Doctrine and Life* (50:10, December 2000).

Orla O'Toole:

> What the survey indicates about young people's attitudes would match my own experience – that being a Catholic is regarded by many young people in Ireland as their religious heritage: it is a part of what they are. Religion does indeed shape their moral decision-making; but many do not view morality primarily in sexual terms. The belief that a person's sexual behaviour is their own business as long as it does not harm others, is widespread.[9]

Donal Harrington:

> Disaffection with the Church's sexual teaching is at root a
> problem about leadership. Ever since the watershed of *Humanae
> Vitae*, growing numbers of Catholic adults have become
> increasingly incredulous about their Church's teachings on
> sexuality. More and more have come to sense the gap between
> what the Church says and the wisdom arising from their own
> experience.[10]

Anne Thurston:

> My generation had such difficulty in shaking off the shackles of
> repression and guilt in regard to sex that we became deaf to
> anything the Churches had to say.
>
> I suggest that, on the basis of this survey, one of the crying
> needs is for a renewed sexual ethic, one which speaks to people's
> lived experience, one which responds to people's deepest need
> for relationship, one which takes account of same-sex
> relationships, and so on.[11]

Sociologists Christopher Whelan and Niamh Hardiman, writing on
Changing Values in Ireland concluded:

> Many of the younger, more educated sectors of the population,
> particularly in urban areas, are likely to move away from
> religious involvement altogether. Many more of them may well
> continue to be religiously active, as there is evidence of the
> enduring importance of spiritual values in the lives of
> individuals. However they are likely to be less tolerant of
> traditional hierarchical authority and more committed to the
> role of individual choice in moral decision-making.[12]

Images of the World and Happiness

Images of the world in Ireland

There was an optional question which asked about images of the world on a scale from 1, which was 'The world is basically filled with evil and sin' to 7, which was 'There is much goodness in the world which hints at God's goodness'. In Ireland 2 per cent chose '1', 5 per cent chose '2', 11 per cent chose '3', 22 per cent chose '4', 26 per cent chose '5', 17 per cent chose '6' and 16 per cent chose '7'.

Happiness of life in Ireland

The very first question on the questionnaire was 'If you were to consider your life in general these days, how happy or unhappy would you say you were?' and the choices offered for the response were 'Very happy', 'Fairly happy', 'Not very happy', 'Not at all happy', 'Can't choose'. The pattern of responses in Ireland was: Very happy (44 per cent), Fairly happy (51 per cent), Not very happy (5 per cent), Not at all happy (1 per cent).

Differences between age groups were small and not significant, with the exception of the category 'Very happy'. With 44 per cent of all Irish respondents choosing 'Very happy', it was chosen by 51 per cent of the 18-28 year olds and 50 per cent of the 29-38 year olds. The lowest 'Very happy' age group was 59-68 at 33 per cent. Those aged 39-48, 49-58 and 69 and over were similar at 42 per cent, 43 per cent and 43 per cent.

When the responses 'Very happy' and 'Fairly happy' were taken together there was no significant difference between the age groups. The percentage for the 18-28 year olds was highest at 98 per cent and it decreased gradually to 94 per cent of those 69 and older. Similarly, there was not a significant difference across the age groups in the percentages choosing the response 'Not at all happy'. The range was from 0 per cent to 2 per cent.

There was very little variation between age groups for the response 'Not very happy'. The younger age groups 18-28 and 29-38 were slightly less likely to choose this answer at 2 per cent, while those aged 39-48 and 49-58 were similar at 7 per cent and 6 per cent, as were those 59-68 and 69 and over at 5 per cent.

Images of the world internationally
In the twelve countries in which the question on images of the world was asked the pattern of responses for those above the centre point, that is towards there is much goodness in the world which hints at God's goodness, was: **Ireland** (61 per cent), USA (52 per cent), Canada (48 per cent), New Zealand (46 per cent), The Philippines (43 per cent), Latvia (40 per cent), Hungary (36 per cent), Slovakia (29 per cent), Bulgaria (27 per cent), Czech Republic (27 per cent), Portugal (12 per cent), and Russia (8 per cent).

Happiness of life internationally
Internationally, the pattern of the responses 'Very happy' was: The highest was **Ireland** (44 per cent) and next highest were **Northern Ireland** (38 per cent) and the USA (37 per cent), followed by New Zealand (33 per cent), Great Britain (32 per cent), Denmark (32 per cent), the Netherlands (31 per cent), and Australia (30 per cent). Then, in descending order: Switzerland, the Philippines, Chile, Canada, Israel, Sweden, Austria, Norway, Cyprus and Portugal (from 29 per cent to 20 per cent); Spain, Poland, former West Germany, Japan, France and Italy (from 19 per cent to 12 per cent); former East Germany, Slovenia, Czech Republic, Bulgaria, Slovakia, Hungary, Russia and Latvia (from 9 per cent to 5 per cent).

When the response 'Fairly happy' was added to 'Very happy' the pattern changed, except for **Ireland,** which remained the highest, now at 95 per cent. Then came the Netherlands, Australia and Northern Ireland at 94 per cent. Then, in descending order, were: Great Britain, New Zealand, Switzerland, Denmark and USA (from 93 per cent to 90 per cent); Norway, Japan, Spain, Sweden (from 89 per cent to 86 per cent); former West Germany, Canada, Poland, the Philippines and Czech Republic (from 84 per cent to 80 per cent); France, Italy, Israel, Cyprus and former East Germany (from 79 per cent to 70 per cent);

Slovenia and Slovakia (from 69 per cent to 65 per cent); Chile, Portugal, Russia and Bulgaria (from 60 per cent to 54 per cent); Hungary (50 per cent), Latvia (49 per cent).

Some concluding thoughts for discussion
Seán MacRéamoinn, commenting on the Preliminary report on the ISSP data, wrote:

> It may be useful to recall the important distinction between *secularisation* and *secularism*: roughly speaking, the latter denotes a system or world-view which has no place for the transcendent, the supernatural, the divine, while the former is that process by which human life in both personal and social aspects is 'liberated' from the detailed control of *religion*, while remaining lit and guided by faith. Secularism then is a matter of *autonomy* (as distinct from independence), and, far from being inimical to Christian discipleship or mission, may bring both to maturity, as well as opening the mind and will to Christian teaching and tradition.[13]

Michael Paul Gallagher, SJ, a former member of The Pontifical Council for Culture, commented:

> What we need is a richer and converging spirituality for living in our culture and building structures of faith. Such a spirituality would echo some of the great mysteries: Incarnation (embracing cultural realities with hope), Redemption (discerning them and transforming them with love) and Pentecost (having faith in the guidance of the Spirit towards unity-in-diversity).[14]

Andrew Greeley, a world authority on the sociology of religion, who is preparing a study on religion in Europe at the end of the second millennium, maintains that the signs of the times are that religion in

Europe looks stronger than it did at the beginning of the First millennium or the second millennium.[15]

John Henry Cardinal Newman (born 200 years ago) contended that the end of each millennium was characterised by a crisis in the Church and he said the he made his anticipations 'according to the signs of the times' in the society of his day. This was more than a century before the phrase came into use in Church documents.[16]

Epilogue
A poem by Father Brian Power[17]

Waiting With Elijah
Elijah sought the Lord's voice in the storm.
Picture him huddling naked in his grotto
pleading with his God to let him sense
God's nearness and God's need for a servant's mission.
Do we listen for the tapping of a raindrop
or the light murmuring of a gentle breeze
outside our windows? Yet nothing may stir until
we stop expecting; then the divine response
glides towards us in an unexpected phrase
from ageing neighbour or from passing child,
and as night enforces sleep we realise
that God unseen has slipped us his reply.
Let us thank God when he chooses gentle ways
and humble voices to speak to us his servants.

Appendix

A note on methodology
Data available from the ISSP1998 Survey on Religion was organised to suit the perspective of the Irish Centre for Faith and Culture's Conference at Maynooth in June 2001 entitled *Measuring Society:*

Discerning Values and Belief, Religion, Culture and the Social Sciences.
International information was taken from the 32 sets of data currently
available for 29 countries and former West Germany, former East
Germany and Northern Ireland with their separate data sets.

The 32 data sets of the ISSP 1998 Survey on Religion are available,
merged, on a CD, from the Central ISSP Archive at ZA, University of
Cologne, Germany, e mail za@za.uni-koeln.de. Full information is
available at http://www.za.uni-koeln.de/issp The questionnaire used in
the survey is also available there. It is very important for critical
interpretation of the results to check the wording of the standardised
questions used, so that it is possible to see the limitations of the
stimulus which produced a particular response. This has been adverted
to in the course of the paper.

The survey set out to obtain information from a representative
sample of adults about beliefs, patterns of behaviour and attitudes.
Standardised questions were used in all the participating countries, so
that the data obtained would be as comparable as possible. The survey
questions were designed by the International Social Survey
Programme members in 1997, having chosen the theme 'Religion' for
its annual international research project in 1998. The ISSP takes a
different theme each year and when it designed a survey on 'Religion'
it had the advantage of the detached objectivity of the vast majority of
its members and the related disadvantage for this paper that the
questions which it chose to ask do not always adequately tap the
attitudes and imagery of the committed Christian.

In Ireland 1,010 persons aged 18 years of age and over were
interviewed using the Voters Register as a sampling frame. The
interviews were undertaken in May-June 1998 by the Survey Research
Unit of the Economic and Social Research Institute, Dublin. The Irish
sample corresponded to the characteristics of the national population
in gender (47 per cent male, 53 per cent female) and age (17 per cent
18 to 28; 18 per cent 29-38 and 39-48; 15 per cent 49-58 and 59-68;
16 per cent 69 and over). In the categories used by the ISSP, 59 per
cent of the Irish sample said that they were married or living as

married, 10 per cent said that they were widowed, 3 per cent said that they were separated or divorced and 28 per cent said that they were single. Again in the terminology of the ISSP, the current religious denomination Catholic was given by 95 per cent of the sample

The estimated margin of error for a survey like this is not more than plus or minus 3 per cent with a confidence of 95 per cent. Comparisons between age groups are made in this paper only when they appear to be significant having allowed for the margin of error. Percentages in the text of the paper have been given to the nearest one per cent. The percentages were calculated to one decimal place and this sometimes led to an apparent anomaly when separate categories of answers were taken together, e.g. 5.4 per cent appeared as 5 per cent, but if two categories of response at 5.4 per cent were added it became 10.8 per cent, which would appear as 11 per cent. The ISSP-supplied percentages, which are used in this paper, are calculated using the number of respondents who replied to each question as a base. The Preliminary Report in *Doctrine and Life* (50:10, December 2000) was completed before the merged data set was available and calculations were based on the total number interviewed and this occasionally leads to an apparent discrepancy between figures, but the difference does not ever exceed one per cent.

The ISSP CD contains the responses of 39,034 respondents in SPSS format. The data on which this paper was based were extracted by Mairaid Woods, Research Officer in the Social Science Research Centre, University College Dublin, whose efficiency and helpfulness are acknowledged with most sincere thanks.

Notes

1. Dermot A. Lane, *The Experience of God* (Dublin, Veritas, 1985), p. 70.
2. Tony Fahey, 'Religion and Prosperity', *Studies*, 90:357 (Spring 2001), p. 42 and pp. 43-44.
3. Kieran Flanagan, *The Enchantment of Sociology: A Study of Theology and Culture* (London, 1996).
4. *The Irish Times*, February 8 2001, p. 16
5. President Mary McAleese, Address to the National Conference of Priests of Ireland Jubilee 2000 Conference, *NCPI News Bulletin* (Spring 2001), p. 3.
6. Donal Murray, 'Diversity and Religion', *Cultures and Faith*, The Pontifical Council for Culture, Vatican City, 9:1 (2001), pp. 16-32 (p. 19 and p. 23).
7. Liam G. Walsh OP, *Doctrine and Life*, cit. sup., p. 626.
8. David Touhy and Penny Cairns, *Youth 2K* (Dublin, 2000), p. 197 and p. 201.
9. Orla O'Toole, *Doctrine and Life*, cit. sup., p. 654.
10. Donal Harrington, *Doctrine and Life*, cit. sup., p. 646.
11. Anne Thurston, *Doctrine and Life*, cit. sup., p. 636 and p. 637.
12. From the conclusion of Niamh Hardiman and Christopher Whelan, 'Changing Values' in William Crotty and David E. Schmitt (eds), *Ireland and the Politics of Change* (London and New York, 1998), pp. 66-85 (p. 85).
13. Seán Mac Réamoinn, *Doctrine and Life*, cit. sup., p. 658.
14. This is the conclusion of an article by Michael Paul Gallagher, SJ, entitled 'Faith becoming culture: theological perspectives', *New Blackfriars*, 78:913, pp. 111-120 (p. 119). He is described by the Editor as 'an Irish Jesuit who formerly worked in the Pontifical Council for Culture and now teaches theology at the Gregorian University in Rome.'
15. Andrew M. Greeley, *Religion in Europe at the End of the Second Millennium: A sociological sketch*, (Brunswick, New Jersey, Transaction Publications, Forthcoming 2001).
16. From the paper of Bishop Philip Boyce on 'The Enduring Relevance of Newman's Vision of Hope' presented to The Newman Conference of The Pontifical Urban University, Rome, 20 February 2001, reported in *Urbaniana* 2001 and due to be published in the papers of the Conference.
17. Brian Power is a priest of the Dublin diocese. The poem 'Waiting with Elijah' is from his collection entitled *The Past must Rise* (Dublin, 2000).

Different from their Elders and Betters: Age Cohort Differences in the Irish Data of the EVS 1999

As the title suggests this chapter provides a comparative analysis of the Irish data from the 1999 EVS survey from the perspective of age cohort differences. In the course of this study the analysis confirms the widely held viewpoint that the identification of oneself as religious and the time spent in Church is highest in the older age cohorts. In other areas there was very little difference across age. Interestingly, this was evident in responses to the question that asked respondents to rank the importance that they attached to engaging in the social targets listed as the elimination of inequalities, the provision of basic needs for all, and the recognition of people on the basis of their merits. The chapter concludes by acknowledging that there are significant differences between age cohorts on social and religious values. It is not clear, however, whether such changes represent a real alteration over time or simply a generational difference. In this respect, further research is both possible and desirable.

Introduction

The European Values Study is a pan-European project which utilises an omnibus survey focusing especially on values associated with work, religion, lifestyles and other issues. Its most recent data gathering exercise was in 1999, the third of its kind and the first EVS to include former Soviet-bloc countries. Various publications will flow from the data gathered on both an individual and a collective basis in the coming years. This study, however, focuses solely on the EVS data for Ireland from the 1999 study as a stand alone project. Further comparative analysis with previous Irish data will follow but lies outside the scope of the current work.

The 1999 EVS in Ireland had 1,012 completed interviews. It was based on a national random sample population, excluding those under eighteen years of age. Post fieldwork weighting of data by sex, age and educational level was done against the 1997 Labour Force Survey population data. The Irish data for the EVS study were gathered by the Economic and Social Research Institute to whom the author is indebted for access for this paper.

The survey instrument, available online at the EVS homepage, (http://cwis.kub.nl/~fsw_2/evs/info.htm), contains questions on a variety of topics including, but not limited to, attitudes to work, family, friends, politics, leisure, religion, environment, trust, poverty, happiness, citizenship, and immigration. In this paper the focus is on the variation in responses across the age cohorts.

The 1,012 Irish respondents were composed of 498 males and 514 females (Table 1, p. 107), 197 of whom have third level education, and 281 of whom have not completed the first cycle of second level education (Table 2, p. 107).

Table 3 (p. 107) shows the breakdown in ages, with just under 16 per cent of respondents being 24 years of age or less.

In Table 4 (p. 108) a breakdown is given of these age cohorts by educational levels.

The change in educational level across the age cohorts is clear, with the highest level of education amongst the younger groups. This is particularly evident in the column indicating non-completion of the 1st cycle at second level, a category which involves only 1.9 per cent of the youngest cohort (N=3), but fully 68 per cent of the oldest cohort (N=102). There are clear historical reasons for this (for example, access to education), but it is evident that Ireland has an increasingly well-educated population. This paper examines this youngest cohort with a particular focus on how different this group is from the older cohorts.

The EVS instrument asked about the respondent's own statement of personal happiness. Table 5 (p. 109) gives a breakdown of the responses by age. There is no significant difference across the age groups (C^2=19.28, n.s.).

In Table 6 (p. 109) details are given of four contrasting areas relating to ways in which respondents spend their time. It is interesting to note that some 340 (36.3 per cent) respondents spend time in church on a weekly basis or more frequently, with a further 91 (9.7 per cent) stating they do so once or twice a month; but 382 (40.8 per cent) say they never spend time in church. It should be noted that these data are in conflict with the responses given for frequency of attendance at church which will be examined later when discussing Table 13.

In Table 7 (p. 110), the data for time spent in church are examined in detail by age cohort. Here the percentages for never attending are at their highest for the youngest age cohort at 55.9 per cent, closely followed by the 25-34 year olds at 54.8 per cent, figures which contrast strongly with the oldest age group at only 20.1 per cent. Statistical tests suggest that these variables are not independent (C^2=147.19, p <.001.) and modestly negatively associated (Kruskall's g = -0.365, p <.001). The younger the age group, the lower the frequency of spending time in church. Again, the caveat of contradiction with other internal evidence should be noted.

The survey also sought to ascertain attitudes to various social realities such as the type of neighbours one might like, poverty and immigration, as well as looking at religious and spiritual values. It is to these social data that this paper now turns.

The survey asked respondents to indicate whether they would regard persons from specified groups as undesirable neighbours. In Table 8 (p. 110), summary data are given for the percentage of respondents objecting to named groups. The term 'Travellers/Itinerants' is used only in the Irish questionnaire and the result at 50 per cent contrasts strongly with Gypsies at 25 per cent.

Table 9 (p. 111) gives summary data for the total number of unwanted mentions by age. Statistical tests suggest that these variables are not independent (C^2=127.65, p <.001) and weakly associated (Kruskall's g = 0.187, p <.001). Worthy of note is that 50.1 per cent of the youngest cohort mentions three or more categories of unwanted neighbours compared to only 36 per cent of the middle group and 27.1 per cent of the oldest group. Whether this indicates a decreasing level of tolerance in Ireland or is a measure of the relationship between tolerance and age is impossible to say without comparison with data from the previous EVS data sets.

One question asked respondents to identify the reason for people being in need. Table 10 (p. 111) summaries the responses based on the different age cohorts with respondents stating the primary reason, in their opinion, for people living in need. Note the strong contrasts on age between those who choose 'injustice in society' and those choosing 'laziness or lack of will power'. In the latter, only 16.1 per cent of younger people contrasted with 35.2 per cent of the oldest group, whereas in the latter the situation is reversed with 38.1 per cent of the youngest group compared to 26.2 per cent of the oldest group. Cramer's V at .119 was significant, p <.001, indicating a weak level of association between the variables.

Respondents were also asked about their beliefs concerning the favouring of native Irish over immigrants in relation to employment opportunities. The summary data are given in Table 11 (p. 112). Again there is a different based on age with 65.2 per cent of the youngest cohort willing to give priority to native Irish but increasing linearly to 87.2 per cent of the oldest cohort.

Turning to questions of religious practice and values, the survey also sought to ascertain such items as religious identification, church practice, the importance of ritual, attitudes to/belief in God, and frequency of prayer. The summary data for religious identification are given in Table 12 (p. 112). Interestingly, the greatest number of respondents identifying themselves as not belonging to a religious denomination is in the 25-34 years group at 14.4 per cent; in addition the highest percentage of persons identifying themselves as non-denominational now but formerly denominational also belongs to this group, 41 per cent (n=23).

Respondents were also asked to identify their frequency of attendance at religious services. The attendance data crosstabulated with age are given in Table 13 (p. 113). Some 22.8 per cent of the youngest cohort attend weekly or more frequently compared to 85.9 per cent of the oldest cohort. On the other end of the scale 31 per cent of the youngest cohort attend once a year ofr less compared to only 8.7 per cent of the oldest cohort. Statistical tests suggest that these variables are not independent (C^2=316.98, p <.001) and moderately negatively associated (Kruskall's g = -0.491, p <.001). These data are in conflict with the data seen in Table 6, where 40.8 per cent of respondents answered that they spent no time in church; in Table 13 it is clear that 40.8 per cent attend church less than once a week, with only 9.4 per cent specifying 'never' or 'practically never'.

Significantly, despite the wide variation in church attendance, respondents in the different age cohorts answered without much differentiation when asked about the importance of religious rituals at the time of birth, marriage and death, with total numbers of 'yes' in the range of 88.2 per cent to 99.3 per cent as seen in Table 14 (p. 113).

When asked 'Are you a religious person?' the respondents' answers are somewhat different from those given for attendance at religious services, as seen in Table 15 (p. 114). Almost 35 per cent of the youngest cohort identify themselves as not religious compared to about 12 per cent of the oldest group.

When asked about specific elements of belief, interesting patterns emerge, as indicated in Table 16 (p. 114). While 95.8 per cent of all respondents believe in God, only 79.8 per cent believe in life after death, but 85.6 per cent believe in heaven. Belief in sin is quite high at 86.1 per cent but belief in hell is only 53.6 per cent. Generally speaking there is an age-related trend for the traditional beliefs with higher levels of belief in the older cohorts; the opposite holds true for belief in reincarnation and telepathy.

Respondents were asked of the importance of God in their lives on a scale of one to ten, from 'not at all important' to 'very important'. The summary data are given in Table 17 (p. 115). Once again, age is an important factor. In the youngest cohort, those responding on a scale of eight to ten represent 21.7 per cent, a figure which rises linearly through the age cohort to 89.9 per cent in the oldest age group, a moderate level of association (Kruskall's g = -0.435, p <.001).

A subsequent question asked about the frequency of prayer in the respondent's life. The summary data are given in Table 18 (p. 115) and is strongly associated with the importance of God in the previous question (Pearson's r= -.649, bearing in mind the reverse coding of the prayer question). Again a moderate level of association is found (Kruskall's g = 0.449, p <.001).

The survey used a series of item statements measured along a common scale. Respondents were asked to rate a series of actions on a scale of one to ten, where one meant the action could never be justified and ten meant the action could always be justified, with a complete range of possibilities between the two limits. Means and standard deviations are given in Table 19 (p. 116). Divorce and homosexuality are seen as the most justified (the highest means but also the highest

Figure I   **Bar chart of Justification of Suicide by Age by Gender**

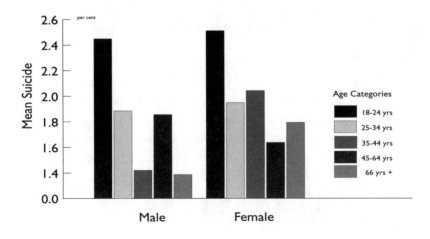

standard deviations) and joyriding as the least justified (smallest mean and smallest standard deviation).

Focusing on one significant issue in the Irish context, that of suicide, it is interesting to examine the data on the basis of both age and gender. Figure 1 (p. 99) represents the answers in graph format.

Table 20 (p. 117) looks at the precise range of responses to the suicide justification question for the 18-25 year olds. There is a significant difference between males and females at the 'never justified' level with 43.2 per cent of males compared to 60.9 per cent of females.

Turning to practical application of values, the survey asks respondents, inter alia, about various targets for the creation of a just society, levels of importance of care for named groups, and willingness to engage in practical expressions of help for specific target groups. The data for the responses are given below in graphic form. In Figure 2 (below) the summary data for three questions are shown. Respondents were asked to state how important it was to engage in each of three social targets: the elimination of inequalities, the provision of basic needs for all, and the recognition of people on the basis of their merits. The scale used was one to five, with one meaning 'not at all important' and five meaning 'very important'. The upward trend in importance based on age can be seen. The basic needs item is not statistically different across the age cohorts. The summary Anova data are seen in Table 21 (p. 117).

**Figure 2   Clustered Bar chart of Age by Social Targets Table 21
                    Summary ANOVA data for Social Targets**

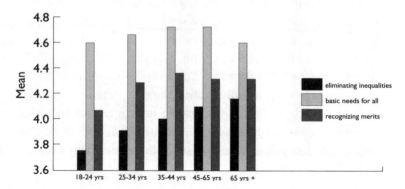

Figure 3 (below) and Table 22 (p. 117) show the corresponding results for a series of 'concern' items, scored in the opposite direction, such that lower scores indicate higher levels of concern. The differences between the groups are least in terms of concern expressed for immigrants, and such concern is the lowest of all.

Figure 3   **Clustered Bar chart of Age by Concern Items Table 22 Summary ANOVA data for Concern Items**

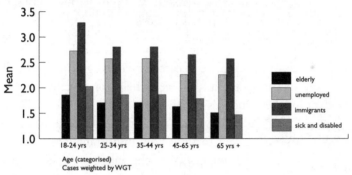

Age (categorised)
Cases weighted by WGT

The same questions were also asked in relation to other groups. Similar summary data are given in Figure 4 (p. 102) and Table 23 (p. 118). In these variables, it is the level of concern for Europeans alone that exhibits differences within the age cohorts, with the youngest group being significantly different from the two oldest groups. On all other variables there were no significant differences across the age groups.

Finally, in this section, respondents were asked about their willingness to give practical expression to their concerns by way of a measure of 'willingness to help' scored with a scale where one means absolutely yes and five absolutely no. Summary data are given Figure 5 (p. 103) and Table 24 (p. 118). There is no disagreement within the age cohorts in respect of immigrants; the data here are closest to the mid-point choice of 'maybe yes, maybe no'. Interestingly, the oldest age cohort is least willing to help immediate family members. The two youngest age groups have the lowest willingness to help the sick and disabled.

From all of the foregoing data it is possible to construct a series of indices which serve as useful summaries for specific trends in the data. There are four such indices.

- 'Liberal' index was created by adding the 'moral act justification' variables together excluding the suicide item. There were 21 items in the index with an alpha of 0.85;
- 'Religiosity' was created by summing the 'yes/no' religious variables together. There were 12 items in the index with an alpha of 0.82;
- 'God' index was computed by adding the 'frequency of practice', 'frequency of prayer' and 'sense of God' variables together. The nature of the three variables suggests a 'God' dimension and had an alpha of 0.78; and, last of all,
- 'Care' index was created by adding the 'concern about' variables together. The nature of the 10 variables suggests a 'Care of Others' dimension and had an alpha of 0.90.

Figures 6 (p. 104) and 7 (p. 105) show the four indices with raw age scores and categorised age cohorts respectively. It should be noted that the direction of the concern items has been reversed for this index such that a high score now means greater concern.

The trends are indicated more obviously in Figure 7 but Figure 6 is a good indicator of the variability within the data. Looking at Figure

Figure 4   **Clustered Bar chart of Age by Concern Items 2 Table 23 Summary ANOVA data for Concern Items 2**

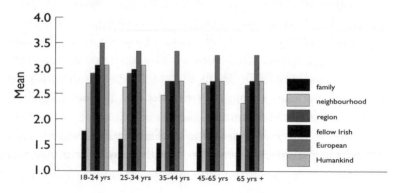

Figure 5   **Clustered Bar chart of Age by Help Items   Table 24 Summary ANOVA data for Help Items**

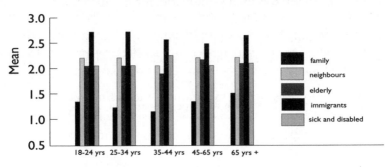

Age (categorised)

7 it is clear that the older cohorts have higher scores on the Care, Religiosity, and God indices and lower scores on the Liberalism index. It should be noted that the level of variation across the age cohorts is greater in the Liberalism and God indices and much less in the others two, Religiosity and Care.

The inter-index correlations in Table 25 (p. 119) indicate a not-unexpected set of results. The Liberalism index is significantly negatively correlated with the Religiosity, Care and God indices. The latter three are significantly correlated with each other, with the correlation between the God index and the Religiosity index being the strongest.

Taking the correlation analysis a step further, Table 26 (p. 119) represents a correlation comparison of the four index variables with two variables already examined above, viz., respondents' perceptions of personal happiness and of justification for suicide. It should again be noted that the suicide justification variable has been omitted from the Liberalism index to facilitate this analysis. Likewise it should be noted that the happiness variable has been recoded so that the higher the score, the higher the measure of happiness.

From the table it is evident that the justification of suicide variable is moderately associated with the Liberalism index and very weakly associated with the Religiosity and God indices. Similarly, the happiness variable is very weakly associated with the God and Care indices. Examining these data for the 18-25 year old group alone, a different picture emerges as seen in Table 27 (p. 120). Here none of the indices are correlated with happiness. On the other hand the justification of suicide variable remains moderately associated with the Liberalism index and weakly negatively associated with the God index.

Figure 6   **Indices with raw age scores**

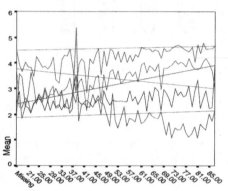

The foregoing tables and charts are a brief introductory review of the Irish data of the European Values Study. In some respects many more questions are raised than answered. From the evidence presented it is quite clear that there are significant differences between the age cohorts on social and religious values, sometimes to a very marked degree. It is not clear, however, whether such changes represent a real alteration over time or simply a generational difference. From anecdotal evidence it would seem reasonable to suspect the former rather than the latter. Other surveys, for example, indicate a clear decline over time in church attendance, something also evident in this survey in terms of generational difference.

Further research is both possible and desirable. It would be a logical next step to evaluate all of the foregoing material in the light of the two earlier EVS datasets for Ireland. Such material has already been made available to the author, courtesy of the ESRI, and the analysis has already commenced, but is outside of the scope of this paper.

More importantly, the data to hand suggest a variety of important social questions which cannot be answered from within the data alone. If religious and social values and attitudes are changing, as strongly suggested here and elsewhere, then what are the implications for Irish society? As we become an increasingly educated society in quantifiable terms, what is happening to our value and belief systems? As those values, attitudes and beliefs change, how will such change be reflected in society? Does the erosion of church practice mean the erosion of religious values or are we simply witnessing transference of allegiance from institutions to self? What about issues like care for others, concern for those in poverty, and the challenge of immigration? The data seem to suggest that such care and concern is decreasing. If so, how will this be remedied such that those in need of care or protection are provided with it? Or is such provision itself under threat?

Is it incontrovertible that Ireland will be different in the future, that the social map will have very different contours, especially in relation to institutional religion. Perhaps we should now be engaged in a formal public debate as to the nature of Ireland in the future. As we let go of things deeply rooted in Irish society, are the prophets of doom correct in foreseeing a complete erosion of values and a descent into mayhem? Or are we simply becoming a mature nation amongst the nations of Europe, whose value and belief systems will simply be more homogenous with our neighbours, who have not fallen apart at the seams?

Figure 7   **Indices with categorised age**

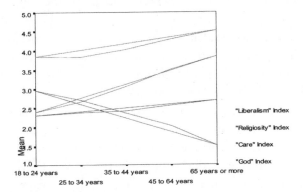

If we choose the latter model, perhaps we might be a little cautious about the future, based on the final two tables relating to justification of suicide, happiness and the various indices created in this analysis. It seems entirely reasonable to suggest that reduction of care and concern for others, a reduced sense of God, and a minimised approach to things religious, allied with a rise in liberalism, are not of themselves harbingers of prosperity and joy for society; the opposite, in fact, seems true, that such a combination results in decreased happiness and increased alienation. As a society how are we to manage change without doing violence to ourselves or others? What price will be paid, and by whom, for our transformation into something different?

Table 1   Frequency Table for Respondent's Sex

	Frequency	Valid Percent
Male	498	49.2
Female	514	50.8
Total	1012	100.0

Table 2   Frequency Table for Respondent's Educational Level in Categories

		Frequency	Valid Percent
Valid	Third Level	197	19.4
	2nd cycle 2nd level	277	27.4
	1st cycle 2nd level	257	25.4
	None/no formal	281	27.8
	Total	1012	100.0

Table 3   Frequency Table for Respondent's Age in Categories

		Frequency	Valid Percent
Valid	18 to 24 years	158	15.6
	25 to 34 years	209	20.7
	35 to 44 years	212	21.0
	45 to 64	282	27.9
	65 years or more	150	14.8
	Total	1012	100.0

Table 4   **Crosstabulation of Age Categories by Educational Level Categories**

*Age (Categorised) *Educational Levels (Categorised) Crosstabulation*

CAT. EDUC.

			Third level	2nd cycle 2nd level	1st cycle 2nd level	None/no formal	Total
Age	18-24 yrs	Count	32	73	50	3	158
		% within Age					
		(Categorised)	20.3	46.2	31.6	1.9	100
	25-34 yrs	Count	66	72	53	18	209
		% within Age					
		(Categorised)	31.6	34.4	25.4	8.6	100
	35-44 yrs	Count	47	60	61	45	213
		% within Age					
		(Categorised)	22.1	28.2	28.6	21.1	100
	45-64 yrs	Count	42	55	71	114	282
		% within Age					
		(Categorised)	14.9	19.5	25.2	40.4	100
	65 yrs +	Count	10	16	22	102	150
		% within Age					
		(Categorised)	6.7	10.7	14.7	68.0	100
Total		Count	197	276	257	282	1012
		% within Age					
		(Categorised)	19.5	27.3	25.4	27.9	100

Table 5   **Crosstabulation of Age by Happiness**

Age (Categorised) *Happiness Crosstabulation

HAPPINESS

			very happy	quite happy	not very happy	not at all happy	Total
Age	18-24 yrs	Count	54	100	4		158
		% within Age (Categorised)	34.2	63.3	2.5		100
	25-34 yrs	Count	91	111	7		209
		% within Age (Categorised)	43.5	53.1	3.3		100
	35-44 yrs	Count	103	102	2	2	209
		% within Age (Categorised)	49.3	48.8	1.0	1.0	100
	45-64 yrs	Count	120	148	11	3	282
		% within Age (Categorised)	42.6	52.5	3.9	1.1	100
	65 yrs +	Count	57	84	8	1	150
		% within Age (Categorised)	3.8	56	5.3	0.7	100
Total		Count	425	545	32	6	1008
		% within Age (Categorised)	42.2	54.1	3.2	0.6	100

Table 6   **Time spent in various situations**

Frequency of time spent with

	friends	colleagues	church	clubs and organisations
na	5	12	12	8
%	0.5	1.5	1.3	0.9
every week	732	213	328	265
	7.2	25.2	35.0	28.7
once twice a month	207	225	91	188
	20.5	26.6	9.7	20.3
few times a year	52	171	122	147
	5.1	20.2	13.0	15.9
not at all	16	218	382	315
	1.5	25.8	40.8	34.1
TOTAL	1012	844	937	924

Table 7   Crosstabulation of Time Spent in Church by Age

spend time in church

	na	dk	every week	once a month	few times a year	not at all	Total
18-24 yrs	1	2	14	22	24	80	143
%	0.7	1.4	9.8	15.4	16.8	55.9	100
25-34 yrs	2		34	17	31	102	186
	1.1		18.3	9.1	16.7	54.8	100
35-44 yrs	1		71	15	33	80	200
	0.5		35.5	7.5	16.5	40	100
45-64 yrs	6		120	26	25	91	268
	2.2		44.8	9.7	9.3	34.0	100
65 yrs +	2		88	11	10	28	139
	1.4		63.3	7.9	7.2	20.1	100
TOTAL	12	2	327	91	123	381	936
	1.3	0.2	34.9	9.7	13.1	40.7	100

Table 8   Percentage of Respondents listing named Groups

Drug Addicts	66	Emotionally Unstable People	25
People with a criminal record	56	People with Aids	23
Itinerants/Travellers	50	Muslims	14
Heavy Drinkers	36	Immigrants	12
Left Wing Exremists	33	People of a different race	12
Right Wing Extremists	32	Jews	11
Homosexuals	27	Large families	9
Gypsies	25		

Table 9   Crosstabulation of Total Unwanted Neighbour Mentions by Age

Total Unwanted Neighbour Mentions

	0	1	2	3	4	5	6	7	8	9	10	11	12	13	14	15	TOTAL
18-24 yrs	16	30	30	26	19	9	7	11	2			3			2	4	159
%	10.1	18.9	18.9	16.4	11.9	5.7	4.4	6.9	1.3			1.9			1.3	2.5	100
25-34 yrs	20	34	32	28	29	15	23	9	5	5	5	1		2	1	1	210
%	9.5	16.2	15.2	13.3	13.8	7.1	11	4.3	2.4	2.4	2.4	0.5		1.0	0.5	0.5	100
35-44 yrs	25	16	34	26	31	21	14	12	10	6	4	1	3	1	2	2	208
%	12	7.7	16.3	12.5	14.9	10.1	6.7	5.8	4.8	2.9	1.9	0.5	1.4	0.5	1	1	100
45-64 yrs	26	28	25	37	32	26	23	26	10	16	10	5		3	4	8	279
%	9.3	10	9	12.3	11.5	9.3	8.2	9.3	3.6	5.7	3.6	1.8		1.1	1.4	2.9	100
65 yrs +	6	16	18	19	13	11	10	9	11	8	4	5	6	7	1	4	148
%	4.1	10.8	12.2	12.8	8.8	7.4	6.8	6.1	7.4	5.4	2.7	3.4	4.1	4.7	0.7	2.7	100
TOTAL	93	124	139	136	124	82	77	67	38	35	23	15	9	13	10	19	1004
	9.3	12.4	13.8	13.5	12.4	8.2	7.7	6.7	3.8	3.5	2.3	1.5	9	1.3	1	1.9	100

Table 10   Crosstabulation of Age by (First stated) Reasons for People in Need

living in need first

	unlucky	laziness or lack of willpower	injustice in society	part of modern progress	none of these	Total
18-24 yrs	30	25	59	27	14	155
%	19.4	16.1	38.1	17.4	9.0	100
25-34 yrs	41	37	66	49	10	203
%	20.2	18.2	32.5	24.1	4.9	100
35-44 yrs	50	41	58	51	6	206
%	24.3	19.9	28.2	24.8	2.9	100
45-64 yrs	68	56	100	46	5	275
%	24.7	20.4	36.4	16.7	1.8	100
65 yrs +	39	51	38	15	2	145
%	26.9	35.2	26.2	10.3	1.4	100
TOTAL	228	210	321	188	37	984
	23.2	21.3	32.6	19.1	3.8	100

Table 11   **Crosstabulation of Age by Giving Irish Priority in Employment**

giving Irish employment priority

	agree	disagree	neither	TOTAL
18-24 yrs	103	44	11	158
%	65.2	27.8	7	100
25-34 yrs	138	53	11	202
%	68.3	26.2	5.4	100
35-44 yrs	159	40	12	211
%	75.4	19.5	5.7	100
45-64 yrs	206	54	17	277
%	74.4	19.5	6.1	100
65 yrs +	129	15	4	148
%	87.2	10.0	2.7	100
TOTAL	735	206	55	996
	73.8	20.7	5.5	100

Table 12   **Summary data for Identification of Belonging to Religious Denomination, currently or formerly belong to a religious denomination**

	yes	no	formerly yes
18-24 yrs	141	17	11
%	89.2	10.8	
25-34 yrs	179	30	23
%	85.6	14.4	
35-44 yrs	193	19	7
%	91	9	
45-64 yrs	267	15	12
%	94.7	5.3	
65 yrs or more	145	5	3
%	96.7	3.3	
Total	925	86	56
%	91.5	8.5	

Table 13   **Crosstabulation of Age by Frequency of Attendance at Religious Services**

attend religious services

	more than once a week	once a week	once a month	christmas/ easter day	other special holy days	once a year	less often	never	TOTAL
18-24 yrs	3	33	41	30	2	16	9	24	158
%	1.9	20.9	25.9	19	1.3	10.1	5.7	15.2	100
25-34 yrs	8	71	28	32	7	20	15	27	208
	3.8	34.1	13.5	15.4	3.4	9.6	7.2	13	100
35-44 yrs	14	115	16	34	3	5	4	21	212
	6.6	54.2	7.5	16	1.4	2.4	1.9	9.9	100
45-64 yrs	57	166	16	10	5	6	1	18	279
	20.4	59.5	5.7	3.6	1.8	2.2	0.4	6.5	100
65 yrs +	5.4	74	7		1	2	6	5	149
	36.2	49.7	4.7		0.7	1.3	4	3.4	100
TOTAL	136	459	108	106	18	4.9	35	95	1006
	13.5	45.6	10.7	10.5	1.8	4.9	3.5	9.4	100

Table 14   **Summary data for Yes responses to Importance of Religious Ritual for Birth, Marriage and Death**

	YES		
	Birth	**Marriage**	**Death**
18-24 yrs	137	146	153
%	88.40	94.20	99.35
25-34 yrs	180	181	195
%	88.20	87.40	93.30
35-44 yrs	189	190	198
%	89.20	90	93.83
45-64 yrs	256	259	268
%	93.10	94.20	96.05
65 yrs or more	145	147	149
%	97.30	98.70	99.33
TOTAL	907	923	963
%	91.2	92.6	96.01

Table 15 **Crosstabulation for Age by Identification of Self as Religious**

Are you a religious person?

	Religious person	not religious person	convinced atheist
18-24 yrs	97	53	2
%	63.8	34.9	1.3
25-34 yrs	131	60	7
%	66.2	30.3	3.5
35-44 yrs	146	54	7
%	70.5	26.1	3.4
45-64 yrs	218	54	1
%	79.9	19.8	0.4
65 yrs or more	129	18	
%	87.8	12.2	
TOTAL	721	239	17
	73.8	24.5	1.7

Table 16 **Summary data for Yes responses to Belief Items by Age**

Yes responses for Elements of Belief

	belief in God	belief in life after death	belif in hell	belief in heaven	belief in sin	belief in telepathy	belief in reincarnation
18-24 yrs	146	99	63	123	119	64	37
%	94.80	70.7	42.60	83.1	83.2	50.4	28.2
25-34 yrs	186	127	92	139	160	77	44
%	92.5	70.2	51.4	75.1	82.5	44.8	26.2
35-44 yrs	197	133	77	153	162	59	45
%	93.8	80.1	44.5	83.2	86.2	36.9	24.9
45-64 yrs	271	208	143	228	230	96	59
%	98.2	85.6	60.3	90.8	87.8	45.9	25.3
65 yrs +	149	129	91	137	131	27	15
%	99.3	90.8	68.4	95.8	90.3	23.9	10.9
TOTAL	949	696	466	780	802	323	200
	95.8	79.8	53.6	85.6	86.1	41.4	23.5

Table 17   Crosstabulation of Age by Importance of God in Life

Importance of God in life

	not at all	2	3	4	5	6	7	8	9	very	TOTAL
18-24 yrs	12	3	9	10	36	27	26	7	11	16	157
%	7.6	1.9	5.7	6.4	22.9	17.2	16.6	4.5	7	10.2	100
25-34 yrs	15	3	14	13	27	25	25	26	11	47	207
%	7.2	1.4	6.8	6.3	13	12.1	12.1	12.6	5.3	22.7	100
35-44 yrs	7	7	8	16	20	13	26	29	19	68	213
%	3.3	3.3	3.8	7.5	9.4	6.1	12.2	13.6	8.9	31.9	100
45-64 yrs	4	2	5	8	15	19	27	42	28	131	281
%	1.4	0.7	1.8	2.8	5.3	6.8	9.6	14.9	10	46.6	100
65 yrs +	1	1	1	1	3	3	5	20	11	104	150
%	0.7	0.7	0.7	0.7	2	2	3.3	13.3	7.3	69.3	100
TOTAL	39	16	3.7	48	101	87	109	124	80	366	1008
%	3.9	1.6	3.7	4.8	10	8.6	10.8	12.3	7.9	36.3	100

Table 18   Crosstabulation of Age by Frequency of Prayer

Frequency of prayer

	every day	more than once a week	once a week	at least once a week	several times a year	less often	never	TOTAL
18-24 yrs	20.8	15.1	12.6	12.6	4.4	17.6	15.7	100
25-34 yrs	58	27	23	23	24	19	33	208
	27.9	13	11.1	11.1	11.5	9.1	15.9	100
35-44 yrs	81	42	23	18	15	15	17	213
	38	19.7	10.8	8.5	7	7	8	100
45-64 yrs	171	47	18	13	7	11	13	280
	61.1	16,8	6.4	4.6	2.5	3.9	4.6	100
65 yrs +	121	16	6	2	1	2	2	150
	80.7	10.7	4	1.3	0.7	1.3	1.3	100
TOTAL	464	156	90	76	54	75	90	1010
	45.9	15.4	8.9	7.5	5.3	7.4	8.9	100

Table 19   Means and Standard Deviations for Justification Item Statements

	N Valid	Mean	Std Deviation
claim state benefits	990	1.89	1.66
cheating on tax	991	2.34	2.09
joyriding	994	1.12	0.74
taking soft drugs	992	1.94	1.87
lying	987	2.31	1.86
adultery	980	1.82	1.63
accepting a bribe	988	1.46	1.27
homosexuality	931	4.27	3.17
abortion	976	2.83	2.43
divorce	964	4.76	2.90
euthanasia	933	3.23	2.80
suicide	941	2.05	1.91
throwing away litter	994	1.83	1.59
driving under influence of alcohol	994	1.42	1.19
paying cash	980	2.90	2.36
having casual sex	966	2.66	2.35
smoking in public places	983	3.35	2.58
speeding over limit	994	1.90	1.66
sex under legal age of consent	984	1.47	1.37
prostitution	960	2.54	2.18
experiments with human embryos	937	1.89	1.78
manipulation of food	918	2.01	1.82

Table 20   **Crosstabulation of Sex by Justification of Suicide for 18-25 year olds**

	never	2	3	4	5	6	7	8	always
				Suicide					
MALE	32	11	11		13		5	2	
	43.2	15	15		18		7	2.7	
FEMALE	42	7		3	7	7	2		1
	60.9	10		4.3	10	10	3		1.4
TOTAL	74	18	11	3	20	7	7	2	1
	51.7	13	7.7	2.1	14	4.9	5	1.4	0.7

Table 21   **Summary ANOVA data for social targets**

eliminating inequalities	3.789	0.005
basic needs for all	2.150	0.073
recognising merits	2.776	0.026

Table 22   **Summary ANOVA data for concern items**

	F	Sig
concerned with elderly	4.297	0.002
concerned with unemployed	3.932	0.004
concerned with immigrants	2.467	0.043
concerned with sick and disabled	8.295	0.000

Table 23   **Summary ANOVA data for concern items 2**

	F	Sig
family	1.048	0.381
neighbourhood	1.864	0.115
region	1.855	0.116
fellow Irish	1.981	0.095
Europeans	3.198	0.013
Humankind	1.272	0.279

Table 24   **Summary ANOVA data for Help Items**

	F	Sig
help immediate family	5.740	0.00
help people in neighbourhood	5.233	0.00
help elderly	2.070	0.083
help immigrants	1.813	0.124
help sick and disabled	2.932	0.020

Table 25   Inter Index Correlation Matrix

		'Liberalism' Index	'Religiosity' Index	Care Index	'God' Index
'Liberalism' Index	**Pearson Correlation**	1.000	-0.356*	-0.144*	-0.457*
	Sig. (2-tailed)	000	000	000	000
	N	813	542	790	810
'Religiosity' Index	**Pearson Correlation**	-0.356*	1.000	-0.174*	-0.762*
	Sig. (2-tailed)	000	000	000	000
	N	542	607	586	606
'Care' Index	**Pearson Correlation**	-0.144*	-0.174*	1.000	-0.183*
	Sig. (2-tailed)	000	000	000	000
	N	790	586	973	965
'God' Index	**Pearson Correlation**	-0.457*	-0.762*	-0.183*	1.000
	Sig. (2-tailed)	000	000	000	000
	N	810	606	965	1003

**. Correlation is significant at the 0.01 level (2-tailed)

Table 26   Reduced correlation matrix for Indices with Happiness and Suicide Justification

	happiness	suicide
'Liberalism' Index	-0.49	0.519*
	0.159	000
	811	813
'Religiosity' Index	0.040	-0.104*
	0.323	0.012
	605	587
'Care' Index	0.093*	-0.006
	0.004	0.863
	968	908
'God' Index	0.132*	0.184*
	000	000
	997	933

*. Correlation is significant at the 0.05 level (2-tailed)

**. Correlation is significant at the 0.01 level (2-tailed)

Table 27 **Reduced correlation matrix for Indices with Happiness and Suicide Justification, 18-25 year old Respondents only**

	happiness	suicide
'Liberalism' Index	-0.29	0.514
	0.743	000
	131	131
'Religiosity' Index	-0.004	-0.015*
	0.973	0.890
	93	87
'Care' Index	0.099*	-0.042
	0.222	0.620
	155	144
'God' Index	0.043	-0.212
	0.595	0.010
	157	144

PART II

Measuring Society:
Discerning the Ethical World
of the Social Sciences

Models of Man:
Transcendence
and Being-in-the-World[1]

MARGARET S. ARCHER

*Two 'models of man' have dominated Social Theory since the
Enlightenment, privileging atheism because of their respective
anthropocentricism and sociocentrism. These conceptions of 'Modernity's
Man' and 'Society's Being' are considered defective for social science and for
faith alike. A counter-model is advanced from the Realist perspective. In
it, what human subjects become derives from the interplay between their
biological potentials and their practical interactions with the real world.
In secular terms, their relations with nature, practice and society determine
their being-in-the-world. The justification for restricting reality to these
naturalistic orders and excluding Transcendental reality is then questioned.
Religious experience is defended as affecting our being-in-the-world by
reference to two unique effects (feelings of sinfulness and detachment),
proper to those who make Transcendence their 'ultimate concern'.*

Introduction

Throughout their history the social sciences have privileged atheism.
They are an extended example of the general asymmetry between the
need to justify faith, and the assumption that atheism supposedly
requires no such justification. Indeed, social science bears much
responsibility for enabling atheism to be presented as an

epistemologically neutral position, instead of what it is, a commitment to a belief in the absence of religious phenomena. In part, this derives from the personal irreligiosity of its founding fathers; Durkheim and Marx became prominent 'masters of suspicion', whilst Weber declared himself 'religiously unmusical'. In equal part, it can be attributed to the pervasive methodological endorsement of empiricism which illegitimately confines investigation to observables. At best, empiricists consigned non-observables to the metaphysical realm, at worst, logical positivists deemed them 'nonsense', and, in sum, they confirmed the hegemony of sense data over everything that can be known. Since realism has mounted such a remorseless critique upon empiricism, it is overdue that only now do we turn to ousting its bedfellow, atheism.

Until recently, it was commonplace for observers to hold that progress in natural science was accountable for the 'God of the Gaps', with divinity keeping only a shrinking toehold where scientists had not yet trod. Yet, modern scientists themselves are less inclined to view their endeavours in this zero-sum manner. They seem more disposed to admit that their findings do not contradict the majority of theistic beliefs, with the exception of literal fundamentalism. Because nothing in the current enterprise of natural science ultimately hangs upon the presumption of atheism, more of its practitioners endorse the intellectually respectable position of agnosticism, while some actively explore the compatibilities between science and religion. This realisation appears to come early in scientific apprenticeship; it seems no accident that students of natural and applied science are over-represented in our university chaplaincies, compared with social science students. Nor is it circumstantial that within sociology my believing colleagues can be counted on one's fingers; for much does hang upon atheism in the social sciences, particularly the very concept of the human subject. The less he or she is held to be exclusively the subject of social forces, then the more an unwanted modesty is enforced upon these imperialistic disciplines. Thus, Alston appears to be correct in pinpointing the human sciences as the major adversaries of religion, precisely because of their concept of humanity.

I cannot see that there are any contradictions between established scientific results and central Christian doctrines ... I will not go so far as to maintain that there *can* be no contradiction between scientific results and central tenets of Christianity. *The most obvious possibility concerns the human sciences.* It undoubtedly is crucial for theistic religion that it work with a conception of man as capable of being addressed by God, capable of freely deciding whether or not to follow God's behests, capable of eternal loving communion with God after the death of the body. And some views about human nature do not allow for any such possibilities.[2]

He restricts his case to the examples of behaviourism and psychoanalysis.

I want to go much further than this and to make two additional points. Firstly, the argument will be presented that from the Enlightenment onwards, 'models of man'[3] have systematically precluded the human subject from having transcendental relations, and have assimilated historical and comparative evidence about the extensiveness of religiosity to exclusively social causes. Here, it will be maintained that such conceptions of humanity are defective for social science and for faith alike. Secondly, the bulk of the argument will be concerned with how the realist conception of the human being is both superior for social science, but simultaneously makes space for human relations with the divine, which are not ruled out in advance.

Modernity's Man and Society's Being

To begin with the first point: two defective models of the human being have sequentially dominated social theorising since the Enlightenment. These are mirror images of each other, since the one stresses complete human self-sufficiency, whilst the other emphasises utter social dependency.

In cameo, the Enlightenment had allowed the 'death of God' to issue in titanic man. Thus, with the secularisation of modernity went a progressive endorsement of human self-determination, of people's powers to come to know the world, master their environment and thus to control their own destiny as the 'measure of all things'. This lies at the heart of secular humanism, a tough anthropocentric doctrine that nothing matters at all except in so far as it matters to man, which is not to be confused with humaneness.[4]

Not only does 'Modernity's Man' stand outside nature as its master, he also stands outside history as the lone individual whose relations with other beings and other things are not in any way constitutive of his self, but are merely contingent accretions, detachable from his essence. Thus the modern self is universally pre-given. Because all that is contingent can be stripped from this self, he can step forward as a purely logocentric being whose consciousness, freed from any embedding in historical circumstances, can pellucidly articulate the cosmic story. The metaphysics of modernity thus adduced a model of rational man who could attain his ends in the world by pure logos; this was a disenchanted world made up of natural and social reality alone, for it had been ontologically purged of Transcendence.

As the heritage of the Enlightenment tradition, 'Modernity's Man' was a model which had stripped down the human being until he had one property alone, that of instrumental rationality, namely the capacity to maximise his preferences through means-ends relationships and so to optimise his utility. Yet, this model of *homo economicus* could not deal with our normativity or our affectivity, both of which are intentional, that is they are 'about' relations with our environment: natural, practical, social and transcendental. These relationships could not be allowed to be, even partially, constitutive of who we are. Instead, the lone, atomistic and opportunistic bargain-hunter stood forth as the impoverished model of man. On the one hand, some of the many things social with which this model could not deal were phenomena like voluntary collective behaviour, leading to the creation of public goods; or normative behaviour, when *homo economicus* recognised his dependence upon others for his own welfare; and, finally, his expressive solidarity and willingness to share. All of these deficiencies remained, despite tortuous efforts to dismantle the notion of altruism altogether, and thus to reduce seemingly altruistic behaviour to first-order self interest or to second-order advantages accruing to 'inclusive kin'. On the other hand, one of the most important things with which this model could not cope is the human capacity to transcend instrumental rationality and to have 'ultimate concerns'. These are concerns that are not a means to anything beyond them, but are commitments which are constitutive of who we are, and an expression of our identities. Who we are, is a matter of what we care about most. This is what makes us moral beings. It is only in the light of our 'ultimate concerns' that our actions are ultimately intelligible. None of this caring can be impoverished by reducing it to an instrumental means-ends relationship, which is presumed to leave us 'better off' relative to some indeterminate notion of future 'utility'.

However, this was the model of man that was eagerly seized upon by social contract theorists in politics, Utilitarians in ethics and social policy, and liberals in political economy. *Homo Economicus* is a survivor. He not only lives on as the anchorman of microeconomics and the hero of neo-liberalism, but he is also a colonial adventurer and, in the hands of Rational Choice theorists, he bids to conquer social science in general. As Gary Becker outlines this mission, 'The economic approach is a comprehensive one that is applicable to all human behaviour'.[5] True to the Enlightenment tradition, Becker includes human religiosity in this explanandum.[6] The recent burgeoning of Rational Choice Theory in American sociology of religion[7] depends upon the commodification of religion. In the USA, market competition is held to keep the vitality of organised religion high (in contrast to shrinking rates of participation in Europe), as complacent religious organisations cede their positions to the marketeering of thrusting new competitors. Such commodification of religion probably goes some way to explaining the lunar *Landscapes of the Soul* documented by Porpora:[8] we do not find the meaning of life in the conservatories, cruises and consumables which are successfully marketed to us, so why should it be found through denominational marketeering?

However, the rise of postmodernism during the last two decades, represented a virulent rejection of 'Modernity's Man', which then spilt over into the dissolution of the human subject and a corresponding inflation of the importance of society. This displacement of the human subject and this celebration of the power of social forces to shape and to mould, reaches back to the Durkheimian view of the human being as 'indeterminate material'. Now, in Lyotard's words, 'a *self* does not amount to much',[9] and in Rorty's follow-up, 'Socialisation ... goes all the way down'.[10] To give humankind this epiphenomenal status necessarily deflects all real interest onto the forces of socialisation, as in every version of Social Constructionism. People are indeed perfectly uninteresting if they posses no personal powers which can make a difference.

The de-centering of the Enlightenment concept of the human being thus leads directly to an actual dissolution of the self. Instead human subjects become kaleidoscopically shaped by the flux of historico-cultural contingencies. References to the human being become indefinite, since contingency deprives him or her of any properties or powers which are intrinsic to humankind and inalienable from it. Consequently, to Foucault, 'Man would be erased, like a face drawn in sand at the edge of the sea'.[11] Postmodernism has massively reinforced the anti-realist strand of idealism in social theory and thus given ballast to Social Constructionism. This is the generic view that there are no emergent properties and powers pertaining to human agents, that is ones which exist between human beings as organic parcels of molecules and humankind as generated from a network of social meanings.[12] The model of 'Society's Being' is Social Constructionism's contribution to the debate, one which presents all our human properties and powers, beyond our biological constitution, as the gift of society. From this viewpoint, there is only one flat, unstratified, powerful particular – the human person, who is a site, or a literal point of view. Beyond that, our selfhood is a grammatical fiction, a product of our learning to master the first-person pronoun system, and thus quite simply a theory of the self which is appropriated from society. Constructionism thus elides the concept of self with the sense of self; we are nothing beyond that which society makes us, and it makes us what we are through our joining society's conversation. 'Society's Being' thus impoverishes humanity, by subtracting from our human powers and accrediting all of them – selfhood, reflexivity, thought, memory, emotionality and belief – to society's discourse.

What makes actors act has now become an urgent question because the answer cannot be given in terms of people themselves, who have neither the human resources to pursue their own aims nor the capacity to find reasons good if they are not in social currency. Effectively this means that the Constructionists' agent can only be moved by reasons *appropriated* from society, and thus is basically a conventionalist, in religion as in everything else. Yet, the objection remains that a real 'self' is still needed as a focus for such principles and that an 'over-socialised' self remains inadequate as a locus of their origins and their frequent unconventionality. Constructionism is unable to explain why some people seek to replace societies' rules and unwilling to allow that this originates in people themselves, from their own concerns, forged in the space *between* the self and reality as a whole.

Neither of these two models can capture the 'man of faith', who is responsive to sacred revelation or tradition. Thus, 'Modernity's Man' represents an anthropocentric being, incapable as an 'outsider' of sufficient embedding in a sacred tradition such that this helps to constitute his being-in-the-world, and closed against revelation by his human self-sufficiency, which means that divinity will always be reduced by him to the anthropomorphic: ideal typically to the Goddess of Supreme Reason. Conversely, Society's Being is so sociocentric that he is swamped by tradition (form of life, language-game, etc.), thus lacking the wherewithal to elaborate upon it, and is only open to revelation in so far as it is mediated to him by society. Anthropocentric 'Modernity's Man' makes God and his society in his own image. Sociocentric 'oversocialised' man lets society make him and his God.

Realism's Self

From the realist point of view,[13] the central deficiency of these two models is their basic denial that the nature of reality makes any difference to the people that we become, or even to our becoming people. Modernity's Man is pre-formed, and his formation, that is the emergence of his properties and powers, is not dependent upon his experiences of the world. Indeed, the world can only come to him filtered through an instrumental rationality which is shackled to his interests, whose genesis is left mysterious. Preference formation has remained obscure, from the origins of the Humean 'passions' to the goals optimised by the contemporary rational chooser. The model is anthropocentric, because man works on the world, but the world does not work upon man, except by attaching risks and costs to the accomplishment of his pre-formed designs. In short, he is closed against any experience of reality which could make him fundamentally different from what he already is.

Similarly, Society's Being is also a model which forecloses direct interplay with reality. Here the whole of the world comes to people as sieved through one part of it, 'society's conversation'. Their very notion of being selves is merely a theory appropriated from society, and what they make of the world is a matter of permutation upon their appropriations. Once again, this model cuts man off from any experience of reality itself, which could make him fundamentally different from what social discourse makes of him. Society is the gatekeeper of reality and therefore all that we become is society's gift because it is mediated through it.

What is lost, in both versions, is the crucial notion of experience of reality; that the way the world is can affect how we are. This is because both anthropocentricism and sociocentrism are two versions of the 'espistemic fallacy', where what reality is taken to be, courtesy of our instrumental rationality or social discourse, is substituted for what the world really is. Both models condemn humanity to living out this fallacy, because the gatekeepers they have imposed confine us to mediated experiences alone. Realism can never endorse the 'epistemic fallacy' and, in this connection, it must necessarily insist that how the world is has a regulatory effect upon what we make of it and, in turn, what it makes of us. These effects are independent of our full discursive penetration, just as gravity influenced us and the projects we could entertain, long before we conceptualised it.

In other words, realism opens up a space, which of, course, was never really closed, in which whatever properties and powers pertain to reality can have an unmediated influence upon us, including our (often) inarticulate experiences of them. Primitive man experienced gravity as he fell down inclines and failed to jump over large obstacles, under whatever descriptions, if any, he knew these limitations. Although it is inappropriate to speak of God 'belonging' anywhere, in a purely conceptual sense he 'pertains' to this space, as do other unobservables such as many scientific entities, like gravity. In both religion and science, people can devote their lives to searching for such unobservables and the grounds for their searching are open to rational discussion. What we do know historically, is that they have neither always been right nor always been wrong. The importance of holding this gap open for reality, which can never be restricted to the known, is that we allow for the possibility of unmediated human experiences which are not pre-judged to be *necessarily reducible* to self-referentiality, as in Modernity's Man, or to social constructions, as in Society's Being. Although we readily allow that any experience or interpretation is fallible, we cannot accept a foreclosure which prematurely restricts that which can be experienced, and thus censors the putative objects of experience that are admitted to our human repertoire, and hence allowed to influence what we become as people.

In fact, because of the 'primacy of practice' in realist accounts of human development, which necessarily eschew the 'linguistic fallacy', unmediated experiences of reality already play a central role. All of our typical human properties and powers only exist *in potentia*. Whether any of them are realised, and which of them are, depends upon our interaction with the world, its properties and powers. These are amenable to our experience, contra the unfolding model of

Modernity's Man. Equally, our specific properties and powers as language speakers are dependent upon prior non-linguistic practice in the world. As Merleau-Ponty maintained, the differentiation between self and otherness, then self and object, and finally, self and other subjects, have to be phenomenally acquired before we are capable of making the distinctions which language presupposes. As Piaget's experiments showed, the acquisition of thought and mastery of the principles of identity and non-contradiction, which are indispensable to communication, are acquired in practice. This being the case, then language can only be learnt after unmediated practice in the world, and it gains its meaning from its relation to this same independent reality. To consider language to be dependent upon reality, rather than reality upon language, is to lift the linguistic portcullis; what we experience reality to be will determine what we talk about in the public medium, and not vice versa, contra 'Society's Being'.

This is all part of the primacy assigned to practice in realism's conception of the human subject, which I have discussed at length elsewhere.[14] What the primacy of practice means, in this context, is that the full gamut of reality can enter into our human constitution and development, provided only that we are capable of experiencing it. Of course, this is not true of everything that is real. Partly this is because of our human limitations – for example, we cannot visit every place in the world or hear the full sound frequencies – and partly it is because of the nature of some real entities or mechanisms, such as distant galaxies or atomic fission.

It will readily be agreed that some of our practices are ineluctable, given the way we are made, the way the world is, and the necessity of our interaction. This is the case for the natural order, the practical order and the social order, given that we have to navigate our environments, acquire certain practical competencies and also social skills, if we are to survive, flourish and develop the potentials of our species-being. Not all of the practices that foster our flourishing are even remotely connected to our survival. Today, surviving is perfectly possible without ever experiencing swimming or horse-riding, without being able to drive a car or work a computer, and without belonging to a family or any association. However, the more people are pegged down to survival practices, the more we would judge them to be leading impoverished lives, not because they lack what is physiologically needful, but because they are lacking in that which is humanly enriching.

Now, probably the majority of people in the world's history engaged or engage in religious practices. As with every other kind of practitioner, they claim that their experiences are belief-forming; in this case that religious experience justifies, at least in part, their belief in God. Without doubt all of our belief-forming practices can be wrong, because all human knowledge is fallible. Thus some people conclude from their encounters with nature that mice are dangerous, others decide from their own attempts that sewing on a button is beyond them, and most people, most of the time, have believed in erroneous scientific theories. Yet what distinguishes religious beliefs is that they are often deemed to be necessarily false because the experiences upon which they are based are automatically discounted. I want to show that making such a distinction is not on for the realist, though it is open to some other philosophies of science: ones which realists have submitted to heavy and sustained critique, especially positivism. The aim is to argue that religious experience is as justifiable in theistic belief formation as are other experiences in their respective domains, before maintaining that it is at least as important as are naturalistic experiences in forming us in our concrete singularity.

The Primacy of Practice and Religious Practice

The primacy assigned to practice in making us both distinctively and recognisably human, as well as in the emergence of our sense of selfhood, is what is particular to the realist conception of the human subject. If this is the case, then we cannot pre-judge which practices contribute to our constitution, although we may eventually succeed in demonstrating that some are more important than others, whether to the development of our generic humanity or to that of our concrete singularity. If this is the case, then dismissal of religious practice, as opposed to submitting it to the same rational scrutiny as any other practice which arguably plays a role in making us what we are, represents a performative contradiction. It is so when the justifiability of belief in the transcendental is forced to stand before the bar of sense-data, and there to be judged inadequate merely because the object to which it points is an unobservable. It is all the more so if certain realists unwarrantedly take features, which are not regarded in realism as being in the least normative for scientific practice, as somehow retaining their vigour for religious practice. The act of dismissal seems to reflect an enduring empiricist stance towards religious practice, which simply involves a category mistake about what kind of practice it is. The awareness of God is not like sense perception, and until we absent this lingering empiricist parallel, it is impossible to show that religious practice is a great deal more like practices which are regularly admitted to be constitutive of our being-in-the-world.

The performative contradiction, which is committed when realists turn empiricist in relation to religious experience, seems to be rooted in confining realism to academic topics, rather than accepting its thoroughgoing applicability to everyday activities. In short, for many, realism does not 'go all the way down'. Because sense perception does remain of central importance in our quotidian living, it is allowed to exercise an epistemic imperialism that contradicts a realist ontology. Inconsistent realists then take their own lack of personal religious awareness as a reason for dismissing its possibility, which becomes decisive when they cannot be so positioned as to experience it. This is domestic Humeanism. It is to adopt, with those like O'Hear, the seemingly 'not unreasonable presumption that if something is objectively real, it will have similar effects on other observers similarly placed'.[15] Yet this is not reasonable at all; it is closed system thinking which disallows that generative powers can be suspended or occluded, and that one of the prime contingencies responsible is the intervention of the properties and powers of observers themselves. Thus, perfect pitch exists in music, but we do not all have the capacity to hear it, or to know when we do not.

In experience, there are no constant conjunctures between emission and reception, so universal reception cannot define the ontological status of transmission. Yet this is how Gaskin defines experience of any externally existing object, amongst which God would number, namely as an 'experience such that any other person rightly and properly situated with normally functioning senses, powers of attention, and a suitable conceptual understanding, will have the same experience'.[16] Since his argument is cast in terms of sense data, he has no difficulty in concluding that religious awareness is not of an externally existing object! Everyday Humeans draw the same conclusion about the source of religious awareness, which is why they are so open to the Masters of Suspicion. These either internalise religious experience as wish-fulfilment or self-compensation (which is where Nietzsche and Freud display the anthropocentricism of Modernity's Man), or externalise it as a social product (which is where Marx and Durkheim adhere to the sociocentrism of Society's Being).

Yet why should we accept the imperialism of sense-data in religion when we do not in science? In the latter case, we readily accept unobservable entities whose causal effects are not manifested as regularities at the level of events which are open to being experienced. Sense-data may be crucially important in everyday life, but nevertheless everyday practice does not conform to Gaskin's proposition either. For instance, a wine-tasting does not mean that enthusiastic amateurs will 'have the same experience' as a *sommelier*, but we do not turn our suspiciousness upon him, but rather turn ourselves towards educating our palates. So why do we not do the same with religious practice, and betake ourselves to refining our spiritual sensibility? Perhaps this is because we accept that there is a proper set of tests at a *dégustation*, such that if a wine-taster detects too much tannin, then there are chemical tests for its measurement. However, the *Meilleurs Sommeliers du Monde* did not become such by following analytical chemists around and assimilating their findings into embodied knowledge. Nor is their role confined to such, for they will also evaluate 'balance', 'bouquet', 'heaviness' and 'length', which are *qualitative* assessments. When the lads at the Lagavulin distillery pronounce that 16 years old is the best time to drink this single malt, they are not making a judgement which can be checked by the analytical chemist; the only test is their agreement which is based upon experience itself.

Yet, this is the case for every kind of experience, including sense perception itself, namely that a practice can only be evaluated on the basis of what that practice has taught. Thus we have to rely upon perceptual beliefs to check other perceptual beliefs, on deductive reasoning to test deductive reasoning, and upon memory to evaluate memory claims and so forth. Any testing involves the same circularity. As Alston puts it, choosing tests is an 'insider job', meaning that 'the practice supplies both the tester and the testee: it grades its own examinations'.[17] Religious practice is in exactly the same position, for it has its own orders of contemplatives. To doubt these proficients whilst trusting the lads of Lagavulin or the Association of Chemical Analysts, is to employ a double standard. More is demanded of religious practice than other practices can deliver. It has to pass its own insider tests plus those appropriate to sense-data reports. Without the checks from other observers, which are characteristic of sense perception, then it is held to be an important defect of religious practice and one which prevents religious beliefs, founded upon religious awareness, from being in a defensible epistemic position.

Again this is empiricist imperialism. In general, we do not suppose that beliefs stemming from one practice must be subjected to the same checks as beliefs from a different practice before the first belief can be accepted as rational. If we did, then empiricism would not survive cross-practice testing; whereas we do in fact conclude that the impossibility of deploying mathematical checks upon perceptual reports is without epistemic significance. Neither, for example, can any item of hermeneutic understanding withstand empiricist cross-checking; its respectability rests upon the intersubjective validation alone of non-observable meanings. This is what is appropriate to religious practice too. Experiential reports are not auto-veridical, but are scrutinised against an accumulated tradition of practice by proficients, who will be no less inclined to deem a religious report to be hysterical than would a doctor in a different context. Given that the reliability of all tests is imperfect, this workable degree of intersubjective consensus amongst religious contemplatives puts them in a different and possibly superior position compared with those areas of experience from which any intersubjective agreement is ruled out. Yet we still form beliefs about our own conscious states, on the basis of introspection, where the checks are internal to the subject and consist largely of her past experience. Indeed, we would be immobilised as reflexive and intentional beings if we did not do so. My being excited or surprised does not depend upon your being so under the same conditions, but neither does this state of affairs question the validity of my feeling this way or the utility of my recognising it.

What all of this points to is the existence of plural epistemologies which arise from the irreducible plurality of belief forming practices. This is why it was maintained that the adoption of an empiricist stance towards religious practice was a category mistake. It reflects an unwarranted hegemony of sense-data against which epistemic claims as disparate as those of mathematics, logic, hermeneutics and introspection could not prevail. These are all sovereign spheres of cognition, which necessarily employ different criteria of justification, drawn from their own domains, in a circular process which is the same for sense-data too. Nevertheless, it remains interesting to ask to which type of practices does religious practice belong? This is not because a type has to have more than one member, for introspection seems to stand on its own, but rather because of the surprising family resemblances which emerge between religious practice and other practices which do not seem to be found problematic.

It belongs to the practical domain, where proficiency requires practice, where acquiring performative competence is a matter of apprenticeship in a tacit skill. What is acquired there is practical virtuosity, where the 'feel for' the task is virtually incommunicable and thus can only be examined in practice itself. The idea of having a 'feel for music' appears to work in a way quite similar to the notion of exercising religious sensibility. Both involve enbeddedness in a tradition, which makes their beliefs about what note or chord to play next something which is rooted in a sense of the appropriateness of responding in just that manner. In neither domain is practice a matter of mimicry, nor is improvisation a case where 'anything goes'. Secondly, the idea of a 'feel for music' gives 'some content to the notion of immanence in the world, by which the world can impose a sense of the things to be done or said, played or sung'.[18] These are both creative responses, because our 'feel for' means that we live in that medium, take our prompts from it and can 'play along' with others who do the same.

Not everyone can immediately 'join in' religious practice, any more than everybody can join a jazz quartet; in both cases it takes an apprenticeship to develop a 'feel for'. It may still be objected that music is a 'respectable practice', because it is ultimately about sense-data, as is demonstrated by the phrase 'developing an ear' and the fact that even without one we can all hear something. However, when Max Weber wrote that he was 'religiously unmusical', a softer reading is that he did not deny there was music to be heard; nor do most people, because a majority report instances of spiritual awareness in various surveys. Perhaps they have effectively 'turned their heads away', which is not how 'to develop an ear'. In other words, perhaps they have been so busy attending to other things that these occluded what could have been followed up. As was maintained at the start, all human properties and powers, which include the ability to acquire any form of practical knowledge, only exist *in potentia*. If and when religious awareness does develop, then the (above) argument, that it shares many features with other practices, raises the question as to whether it plays a special and distinctive role in the personal identities of its practitioners, or if it simply represents one practice amongst others?

Personal Identity and Religious Concerns

Practice continues to enjoy primacy where the formation of our unique identities as particular persons is concerned. I have argued at length elsewhere[19] that because of the way in which we are constituted, the way the world is, and of the necessary interaction between the two, that we cannot be other than *concerned* about reality. This is because the different orders of reality, in which we are ineluctably involved, convey specific imports for concerns that we cannot but heed to some degree, given our constitution. However, as reflexive and evaluative beings, we can accord priority to a given concern and relegate others, whilst still accommodating the latter because we cannot be unconcerned about those reality-relations upon which our wellbeing hangs. It is the importance of what we care about[20] which defines us, but, since we cannot but care, to some degree, for the orders of reality which impinge upon us, then it is the precise patterning of their prioritisation and accommodation which defines the unique personal identity of every individual. I will first sketch this as a purely secular argument about our ineluctable embedding in the natural, practical and discursive orders of reality, and then ask what difference relations with transcendental reality make.

All human beings have to confront the natural world, and their embodiment necessarily confers concerns upon them about their physical wellbeing as they encounter their environments. This concern is embodied in our constitution and, although the imports of nature can be downplayed evalutively, they cannot avoid being viscerally registered nor be ignored completely. Secondly, all people are constrained to live and work in the practical world: necessary labour is the lot of *homo faber*. Performative concerns are unavoidably part of our inevitable engagement with the world. The precise objects of our performative concerns are historically and culturally varied, but the import of our competence in dealing with the practical realm is universal. Thirdly, sociality is also and necessarily the lot of human beings, who would be less than what we understand as human without their social engagements. Participation in the social realm entails concerns about self-worth which cannot be avoided in this discursive environment. We cannot evade becoming a subject among subjects, and with this come 'subject referring properties',[21] such as admirable and shameful, which convey the import of society's normative system to our concern about our social standing. These may be very different concerns, since we can choose to stand in very different places, but these are all equally social and thus the impact of social norms upon our comportment cannot be obviated.

This produces a dilemma for every human being, since most of the time most of us have to live in the three orders of reality simultaneously. Therefore, a task which falls to all is to determine how to deal with imports coming in from the three orders, which take the form of emotional commentaries on our concerns and yet inform us about very different kinds of human concerns: in physical well-being, performative achievement and self-worth. These concerns are real; not to heed the relevant commentaries may be deleterious to them and thus to us, and yet nothing guarantees their compatibility. On the contrary; to heed, for example, our physical fear could well lead to performative incompetence or to social acts of which we are ashamed.

This dilemma can only be overcome if each human being arrives at some *modus vivendi* between their ineluctable concerns – and one with which they believe they can live.

This entails disengaging 'ultimate concerns' from subordinate ones. Such an ultimate affirmation can only be made after evaluating the consequences for self, by taking account of the positive and negative costs to be borne and establishing how much we care. Basically, through an inner dialogue we 'test' our ongoing or potential commitments against our emotional commentaries, which tell us how far we are up to living out the committed life reflective of these ultimate concerns. What we ultimately affirm as being of ultimate concern is both that which we value most highly, but also that which we feel we can live out as a commitment. We are, of course, fallible on both counts: we may make incorrect evaluations about the worthiness of what we have deemed our ultimate concerns to be and we may also be mistaken in judgements about ourselves and our ability to see these commitments through. In either case, these concerns are revisable.

Our personal identities derive from our ultimate concerns, from what we care about most, together with our other concerns, which cannot be discarded but are accommodated to our prime commitment. As Frankfurt put the matter, our ultimate concerns are definitive of us, in that what our commitments 'keep us from violating are not our duties or our obligations but ourselves',[22] what I am calling our personal identities.

Now, what difference is made if our relations with transcendental reality are introduced? Obviously, those who hold that they have justifiable beliefs in the existence of God also consider that they have good reasons for holding relations between humanity and divinity to be as ineluctable as those pertaining between humankind and the other orders of reality. That some disavow any transcendental concern and that still others are heedless of it, has the same deleterious consequence for human well-being as ignoring those of our concerns which are vested in natural, practical and social reality. How can we possibly assert this, since non-believers appear to make out just as well in the world, including often making their way through it with at least as much goodness and generosity as do believers? This is directly entailed by the belief that God is love, the quintessence of unconditional love. That is what He offers us by His nature. To defend my case, I have to adduce some ineluctable human concern which hinges upon our relations with transcendental reality, that is one which it is universally deleterious for us to ignore and one which is intimately related to our flourishing.

There seems to be every reason to advance love itself as this concern. As an emotional commentary, love also signals the most profound human concern in that our fulfilment depends upon our need to love and to be loved. Since antiquity it has been debated what makes this particular emotion different from others. The answer seems to lie not in its intentionality, nor in its cognitive and evaluative characteristics, but quite simply in its indispensability. As Robert

Brown puts it, 'What makes love unusual among the emotions is the human inability to do without it – whether its bestowal or receipt – and the immense amount of satisfaction that love commonly brings to the people concerned ... Only love is both completely indispensable to the functioning of human society and a source of the fullest satisfaction known to human beings'.[23] It follows that the unbeliever does not do without love, as she cannot if it is truly indispensable, and may find it in love of nature, of art or of another person, where only in the last case can it be received as well as given. It remains to try to show that someone who settles for anything less than divine love then damages their potential for fulfilment,[24] in a manner roughly analogous to how the ascetic can endanger his physical well-being through an impoverished diet. It goes without saying that the commitment of the hunger striker has this effect.

To care about anything, enough to make it a matter of ultimate concern, entails two elements. Firstly, there is a cognitive judgement about its inherent worth, which is always fallible. Secondly, there is a deep emotional attachment to it and must be since it would be most strange to say that a person was devoted to X if they felt quite indifferent towards it.[25] The affective element is not fallible; we cannot be mistaken that we love, but nevertheless we can love unwisely by pinning our affections on someone or something of whose worth we cannot give good reason.

Now, if the religious believers' belief is justifiable, then he or she cannot be wrong in their cognitive judgement that God is, by his nature, inherently worthy of the highest loving concern. This is how they have experienced him to be, and it is these experiences which constitute the justification for their religious belief.[26] Indeed, unbelievers would probably concur that were there a God whose nature is that of pure unconditional love, whose intentions towards humankind were that we should participate in it to the fullest, who showed the depths of his love by his incarnation, crucifixion and resurrection, then the judgement about his supreme goodness would not be in doubt. What they doubt is not his putative worth, but his existence. However, were they to become convinced through experience that he does exist, they themselves would admit that previously they had invested their loving in something inherently less worthy and which failed fully to satisfy.

We need to go one step further than this to show that complete human fulfilment depends upon perfect love and that only lesser degrees of it derive from imperfect loves. This is because since Aristotle, in the long running debate about whether we love someone or the qualities that they personify, it seems that on either side we settle for the imperfectly worthy. If we love a (human) person 'for themselves', as is often said, then the qualities that they do instantiate may well leave out some of those which we value highly and it is extremely improbable that this would not be the case. Conversely, if we love someone because they (very nearly) embody all the qualities which we value most highly, we will also have to put up with unrelated characteristics to which we are not wholly indifferent: as with the intelligent, beautiful and virtuous woman who also talks all the time. Only a being whose person and nature are identical, and consists in love itself, is inherently and unreservedly worthy of our highest and unmitigated loving concern. Only God fulfils these desiderata. To be love itself is to love unconditionally, as there is nothing else upon which such a nature can set store without contradicting that very nature. It is also to love unchangeably, since to love less or more would be a contradiction in terms. Of course, consequentiality, conditionality and changeability are the rocks upon which human loving most frequently breaks up; human love does indeed tend to alter when it alteration finds.

However, to return to the believer, what difference does the love of God make to their personal identities? In their acknowledgement of transcendental relations, they find an ultimate concern that is cognitively of supreme worth, if they are justified in their beliefs. If so, then one new item of information that they will have gained from their experiences, as opposed to the teaching tradition which contextualises them, is that they are personally loved. Now, it was argued earlier that to hold anything to be an ultimate concern entailed both cognition and affect. Hence, what is now being asked *is how much we care* about that to which we have cognitively assented, for it is how we respond by loving back (with all our heart, soul, strength and mind ...) which determines its effect upon our identities.

We humans respond by loving God back with a feeble lack of proportionality. The reason why is partly because our transcendental experiences are discontinuous and partly because those other concerns do not go away and we let them get in the way: 'Martha, you worry and fret about so many things and yet few are needed' (Lk 10:41). Mostly, we do not have that kind of trust; our other concerns are indeed ineluctable and generally we act as if only our care for them can ensure our well-being in the other orders of reality. We are as familiar with compromise and trade-off as is anyone else about their purely secular concerns. The rich young man from Mark's gospel has often suffered a rough retelling. It was not that he chose a love of Mammon over that of God, because Jesus loved him for the service he already gave, but rather that he would not do that one thing more which would have shown that God was his ultimate concern. Most of us are guilty of wrong ranking rather than rank wrong doing.

Theosis and Being-in-the-world

Nevertheless, those who have experienced anything of the unconditional love of God cannot fail to care about it at all if, as has been maintained, such love is indispensable to human fulfilment. The response may be unworthy, but that does not mean it is non-existent. *Theosis*, or progressive divinisation, is a process that remains incomplete for the vast majority of us believers during our life-spans. However, given fidelity, it is in process and is increasingly formative of us ourselves. The main *inward* effect of endorsing *any* ultimate concern is that it transvalues our feelings. Such a commitment acts as a new sounding-board against which old concerns reverberate: the emotional echo is transformed. Take something as simple as once having enjoyed a pie and a pint. In the natural order, the newly committed vegetarian may now feel positive revulsion; in the practical order, Olympic competitors may see these as salivating temptation; in the social order, the new executive may consider them beneath his status. In other words, any serious commitment acts as a prism on the world which refracts our first-order emotions, transmuting them into second-order feelings, for affectivity is always a commentary upon our concerns. What I want to argue, in conclusion, is that a religious commitment is constitutive of three new transvalued emotions, which are distinctive of this concern and which differentiate its adherents from those dedicated to any form of secular concern. This affectual transformation is the substantive justification of how transcendental relations are at least as important in forming us as are our naturalistic experiences and secular commitments.

The first feeling which is discrete to those who have experienced God as unconditional love is sinfulness: literally of having fundamentally missed the mark, of our representing a different order of 'fallen' being, or of our intrinsic unworthiness to raise our eyes. Sinfulness is qualitatively different from the emotions attending dedication to secular ultimate concerns; however high or deep these be, when we fall short of them the corresponding feelings are self-reproach, remorse, regret or self-contempt. Even the lucky lover, who declares himself unworthy of his beloved, protests something different, namely that he has hit the mark undeservedly. Conversely, disconsolate swains merely feel disconsolate, not sinful. In their turn, these secular feelings are different again from the emotionlessness of those without any commitment, whose only attitude will be can they get away with whatever they seek to do, which is precisely where cost-benefit analysis rules. Sinfulness is regarded as an emotional commentary which is emergent from relations between humanity and divinity, and is expressive of the quintessential disparity between them.

It grows out of those human emotions, such as remorsefulness and unworthiness, but only through their transmutation. This entails a penitential revaluation of our lives, which develops only as the transcendental commitment, and thus the contrast, deepens. Graham

Greene's whisky priest in *The Power and the Glory* progressively embraces his loss of social self-worth and endorses service of God as his ultimate concern, which leads to his martyrdom. At the start of this transvaluation, he treasures his old photograph, showing the well-fed and well-respected Father with his immaculate flock, at a time when his vocation had seemed to involve little sacrificial subordination of physical and social well-being. As his ultimate concern becomes ultimately demanding, his emotions towards the photo are transformed, and its eventual loss is simply to be separated from a reproachful irrelevancy. The more his divinisation proceeds, the deeper his sense of his sinful nothingness. In Newman's words, 'the truest penitence no more comes at first, than perfect conformity to any other part of God's law. It is gained by long practice – it will come at length. The dying Christian will fulfil the part of the returning prodigal more exactly than he ever did in his former years'.[27] The sense of being a sinner intensifies, whereas the protests of unworthy but lucky lovers fade away as they make good their vows to 'prove themselves'. Growing proofs of divine love may indeed rectify a life, but they simultaneously deepen the feeling of disparity: that whatever we do, we have all fallen short of the glory of God. There seems to be no human equivalent to the affect associated with sinfulness; that the closer we become to our ultimate concern, the further apart and more different in kind we feel ourselves to be.

Secondly, let us consider the growth of detachment. There are always costs to commitment, simply because to promote one concern is to demote others, yet the concerns in question are ineluctable. Generically, our three secular concerns were not acquired at will, they emerged from the necessary interplay between the way we are constituted and the way the world is. Consequently, it takes a considerable act of will to prioritise an ultimate concern because this means the subordination (not the repudiation) of other concerns, by producing an alignment between them with which the subject believes he or she can live. Struggle is therefore generic to human commitment to *any* ultimate concern, because subordinate concerns do have naturalistic legitimacy, they are about different aspects of our well-being and the emotional commentaries emanating from them signal the costs entailed to the person by the priorities which they have reflexively determined.

However, although such struggle is endemic to the crystallisation and confirmation of what we care about most, and thus to our personal identities themselves, the battlefield is very different for the believer and the unbeliever. Secular struggles are basically about sustaining dedication to an ultimate concern *within* the three naturalistic concerns, and involve not letting these three slip out of the alignment which has been determined between them. Poignant regrets and powerful temptations often recur after an ultimate commitment has been made; costs are recurrent and the bill is frequently re-presented. In a purely mundane sense, religious commitment is even more expensive. This is because the struggle of those who have put their transcendental commitment first is that they thereby seek to subordinate all *three* of their naturalistic concerns: physical well-being, performative achievement and social self-worth. Those who try to respond more and more freely to God's unconditional love feel drawn to live in conformity with this supreme good, which explicitly means not being conformed to the world.

Their struggle has always been well understood in the Christian tradition and has been represented as the battle between the two Kingdoms, of earth and heaven or, by extension of the military metaphor, as the battle lines between the 'two standards' in St Ignatius's *Spiritual Exercises*. In our own terms, it is the antinomy and antagonism between transfiguring *theosis* and both the anthropocentricism of 'Modernity's Man' and the sociocentrism of 'Society's Being'. This struggle is constitutive of a new transvalued emotion, detachment. By definition, such detachment is without secular counterpart, precisely because it constitutes a new view of naturalistic reality and a different way of being-in-the-world with its three concerns. Since it is a transvaluation, its secular precursors are emotions such as resignation towards what has been subordinated, as with the careerist, resigned to the loss of his sporting life, or the mother who reconciles herself to putting her career on hold. However, these secular responses of resignation to the consequences of having made an ultimate commitment are negative emotions, tinged with nostalgia, at best, and bitter regret, at worst. It is the absence of such negativity that distinguishes the growth of religious detachment.

Detachment does not mean that the battle is over, for it never is; compromise, concession and betrayal are life-long possibilities and assailants. Yet, in the lulls, detachment is a new and positive commentary upon being in the world, but not of it. Detachment is a real inner rejoicing in the freedom of unwanting; it is a carefree trusting that all manner of things will be well; it is the ultimate celebration of being over having or not-having. It is the feeling that we are *sub specie aeternitatis* and have been unbound from the wheel; freed from those heteronomous determinations of body, labour and self-worth, and glimpsed autonomy in the form of sharing in divine autarky. Under the prompting of this emotional commentary, our orientation towards the world is transformed; since our identity is not primarily vested in it, we are enabled to serve it. In disinterested involvement, true detached concern is possible: for the planet, for the good use of material culture, and for the intrinsic value of every human being and encounter. Thus, comportment towards the three naturalistic orders is itself transfigured. If seeking to be conformed to unconditional love is the ultimate concern, then it will be more formative of our way of being-in-the-world than can any other naturalistic commitment.

This is where the argument comes full circle. There are certain ways of being-in-the-world which remain incomprehensible without the admission of transcendence. It has been maintained that there are no good reasons for keeping religious practice out of human being, and that the primacy attached to practice in realism's 'model of man' makes it the only one which can let it in. The relations formed in transcendental 'space' react back upon the world, to which they are not conformed, by sanctifying it. From these relations ripple out concentric circles of unconditional love. Such love is the antithesis of private property; it entails a totalising impulse which reaches out to embrace, and thus to liberate the world, in an upwards redemptive spiral. Thus the *theosis* of our concrete singularity collaborates, combines and coalesces with the universalism of the divine economy. Full human coalescence with the transcendental entails the transformation of the third emotion, mentioned above, where gratitude is transmuted into worship as *theosis* and *kenosis* conjoin. This way of being-in-the-world, for the few who ascend to living in love, who give wholehearted priority to God as their ultimate concern and who are correspondingly generous in the subordination of their secular concerns, would require a detailed examination of the saints and mystics. Full unification with God does come only to the few, but the rest of us need not remain total strangers to His purification and illumination.

Notes

1. Alongside the other articles in this publication, this articles arose from a paper given at the Symposium organised by the Irish Centre for Faith and Culture in June 2001 entitled *Measuring Society: Discerning Values and Beliefs* in St Patrick's College Maynooth. In its present form it is reproduced from Margaret S. Archer, Andrew Collier and Douglas V. Porpora, *Transcendence: Critical Realism and God* (Taylor and Francis, Forthcoming 2002).

2. William Alston, *Perceiving God: The Epistemology* of *Religious Experience* (Ithaca and London, Cornell University Press, 1991), p. 240. (My italics).

3. 'Rational Man' was the term current in Enlightenment thinking. Because it is awkward to impose inclusive language retrospectively and distracting to insert inverted commas, I reluctantly abide with the term 'man', as standing for humanity, when referring to this tradition, its heirs, successors and adversaries.

4. See Kate Soper, *Humanism and Anti-Humanism* (London, Hutchinson, 1986), esp. p. 24f.

5. G. Becker, *The Economic Approach to Human Behaviour* (Chicago University Press, 1976), p. 8.

6.   G. Becker, *Accounting for Tastes* (Cambridge, Mass., Harvard University Press, 1996), esp. Ch 11.

7.   See R.S. Warner, 'Work in progress toward a new paradigm for the sociological study of religion', *American Journal of Sociology*, 98:5 (1993).

8.   Douglas V. Porpora, *Landscapes of the Soul* (Oxford University Press, 2001).

9.   J-F. Lyotard, *The Postmodern Condition* (Minneapolis, University of Minnesota Press, 1984), p.15.

10. Richard Rorty, *Contingency, Irony and Solidarity* (Cambridge University Press, 1989), p. 185.

11. M. Foucault, *The Order of Things* (New York, Random House, 1970), p. 387.

12. The best example of this model is provided by the work of Rom Harré. The leitmotif of his social constructionism is the following statement: 'A person is not a natural object, but a cultural artefact'. *Personal Being* (Basil Blackwell, Oxford, 1983), p. 20.

13. This refers specifically to the modern philosophy of science known variously as 'Critical Realism', 'Transcendental Realism' or 'Social Realism'. See Margaret S. Archer, Roy Bhaskar, Andrew Collier and Alan Norrie (eds), *Critical Realism: Essential Readings* (London, Routledge, 1998).

14. Margaret S. Archer, *Being Human: The Problem of Agency* (Cambridge University Press, 2000).

15. Anthony O'Hear, *Experience, Explanation and Faith* (London, Routledge and Kegan Paul, 1984), p. 45.

16. J.C.A. Gaskin, *The Quest for Eternity* (New York, Penguin, 1984), p. 80 (My italics).

17. William P. Alston, *Perceiving God*, op. cit., p. 217.

18. Michael Luntley, *Reason, Truth and Self* (Routledge, 1995), p. 213. This is Luntley's metaphor for moral judgement; I suspect he will not approve of the uses to which I am putting it.

19. See Margaret S. Archer, *Being Human*, op. cit., esp. Chapters 6 and 7.

20. See Harry G. Frankfurt, *The Importance of What we Care About* (Cambridge University Press, 1988), Ch. 7.

21. Charles Taylor, 'Self-Interpreting Animals', in his *Human Agency and Language* (Cambridge University Press, 1985).

22. Harry G. Frankfurt, *The Importance of What We Care About*, op. cit., p. 91.

23. Robert Brown, *Analyzing Love* (Cambridge University Press, 1987), pp. 126-7.

24. This is basically St Augustine's argument: 'Fecisti nos ad to et inquietum est cor nostrum donec requiescat in te'.

25. See Justin Oakley, *Morality and the Emotions* (London, Routledge, 1992), p. 65.

26. Note that this is an argument *from* religious experience. Those who come to believe in other ways, such as through tradition alone or from natural theology, will not have personal knowledge of God's nature, in the first case, and may not even ascribe a nature to him, in the second case, where he may simply be accepted as a (mechanistic) 'first cause'.

27. Cited in Owen Chadwick, *The Mind of the Oxford Movement* (London, Adam and Charles Black, 1960), p. 153.

Searching for Truth,
Revealing Power,
Hoping for Freedom

Tom Inglis

It is hard to get beyond the post-modern notion that truth is produced within discourses that are historically and culturally constituted and which are consequently arbitrary and relative. And yet there is an interest if not an imperative to search for and announce the truth. For me, this interest in truth is closely allied to an interest in freedom. It is the struggle to challenge and resist existing truths, to tell a different truth. It is about revealing the way power produces truth through discourses which become part of the way we read, understand and interpret the world. Truth, revelation and freedom come from knowing and understanding how power operates. This chapter is a critical reflection as to how this struggle has been part of my work as a sociologist. It examines how the will to truth is compromised by the struggle — by both individuals like myself and institutions such as the Catholic Church — to attain and maintain power. It is, in effect, a reflection on my life and work on Irish Catholicism, sexuality, the state, and the media.[1]

'The vocation of every university is service to the
truth: to discover it and transmit it to others'
(Pope John Paul II: Address to the 6th Centenary of the
Jagellonian University of Krakow)

Introduction

What is the interest in doing sociology? What do sociologists write about and, perhaps more important, for whom do they write? These are some of the critically reflexive questions which preside, often in their absence, in the daily struggle of researching and writing.

The easiest solution would be to stop writing, especially since many outsiders believe that sociologists only produce indigestible theories and statistics. And yet I believe that unveiling and revealing that complexities of social life, which we take so easily for granted, is not only a most difficult task, it can be the most rewarding and liberating. To know and understand how we came to be the way we are, to be able to act freely and independently, one has to critically reflect on the time and conditions within which we have been constituted.

I think that most sociologists want to speak the truth about society. However, I believe that we ought to be on our guard and critically reflective about how we do this. This is because the interest in telling the truth is circumscribed by other interests, and because producing or telling the truth is necessarily enmeshed in relations of power. If we are going to speak the truth, we have to be conscious of power and the way it operates. It is only then that we have any hope of breaking free from the boundaries of existing structures and discourses of power, and the truths that are produced within them.

Sometimes it seems to me that sociologists are some kind of modern-day priests, cultivated within the academy and blessed by the media, to speak the truth about social life. Sociologists are not without power. When we speak, we often do so from a position of authority, as some kind of expert, sanctioned by degrees and publications. And this is the reason we must be vigilant and critically reflective, it is very easy to slip from searching for the truth into announcing it. In this sense, sociologists must realise that they write and speak from a designated social position, as professors, lecturers, researchers, and that it is the position more than the person who speaks that announces the truth. And so the critical reflection about the public role of sociologists, their interests and commitments, should begin by asking who are these people who announce the truth of the world with such certainty and conviction. From what position do they speak? Do they have an objective, scientific understanding of the social world? Do they have a sympathetic, caring understanding for those who suffer under the weight of the world? Or perhaps the question is more complicated than this. Are sociologists not scholastics from a different class and culture, who see, read and understand the world differently? So how can we understand the logic of the everyday lives of the people about whom we announce the truth? Worse still, by announcing the truth about them, do we take the words from their mouth? Have we become part of some highly rational, but ever reasonable system of symbolic domination.[2]

But, at the same time, critical self-awareness of the way we produce truth has to be couched in terms of how sociology as a field or discipline is limited and controlled by other fields, particularly power, and how this prevents or inhibits speaking the truth. Is it possible for sociologists to speak the truth about the Catholic Church without being dedicated, loyal members? What has been the influence of the Church over the way Irish people see, read and interpret the world, and in the way Irish sociologists have sought to question this?

I want to elaborate on these issues by reflecting critically on my own work. What have been the conditions and circumstances within which I have searched for the truth about Irish culture and society. In trying to speak the truth I have concentrated on analysing structures of power and how these have limited and controlled what we do and say, and how we read, understand and interpret the world.

A Will to Power?

I want to begin my critical reflections by asking the opposite question. That is, to what extent are sociologists driven not by a will to speak the truth, but rather by a will to power. To what extent does the interest in doing sociology lie in a will to greater mastery and control of oneself and the world?[3]

This has two dimensions. At a personal level, sociology could be seen like a sophisticated form of pop psychology that enables sociologists to exert power over others. Knowing the nature of social power enables sociologists to get their own way, to be better at mastering and controlling others.[4] In other words, in the same way that knowledge of markets helps analysts make good investments, sociological knowledge of Irish beliefs, values, habits and customs could be seen as an important element in the struggle to manipulate and control others and, at the same to, to attain their honour and respect.

This raises interesting questions about how much sociology is used by sociologists as a form of critical self-understanding. Is it ludicrous to ask if sociologists who study and analyse organisations are better qualified to run them? Should we expect those who study the history of manners to be more civilised? Or that those who study the sociology of food would be good cooks? I do not know the answer, but I believe that sociology is not that practical when it comes to self-improvement and being powerful.

However, this is not to deny that most sociologists are engaged in a strategic struggle to attain position, honour and respect in the field of sociology. Indeed it is because many of us are so consumed with this struggle for recognition and position, that we end up writing more for ourselves and other academics than for the general public. The result is that sociology has developed its own specialist language and logic, which is not just inaccessible to the wider public, but irrelevant.

If sociologists are not driven by a will to personal mastery and control, are they instead consumed with an interest in making the world more rational, controlled and efficient? The unquestioned orthodoxy of many sociologists who engage in social policy research is that their work helps make the world a better place. But often the consequence, perhaps unintended, of such research is that it increases the rational regulation of social life. This maintains the existing social order and reproduces rather than changes imbalances in the distribution of power. This raises all sorts of questions about the extent to which capitalist society can become mature, democratic and civil, to what extent this is dependent on creating and maintaining social welfare states, and the role of sociologists in such states. But rather than trying to answer this enormously difficult question, let me stand back and ask an even bigger one. To what extent should we see the Enlightenment as a project to harness reason to create an ever more rational society?

But rather than talk abstractly about the interests and role of the sociologist, it might be more in keeping with the context and theme of this book for me to reflect critically about my own work as a sociologist. Over the years, I have become interested in issues about power, truth and symbolic domination, but I began my career in policy oriented research.

From Tradesman to Action-oriented Research

My apprenticeship in sociology was in conducting social survey research mainly for the Irish Catholic Church. The objective of this research was to obtain accurate knowledge of the nature and level of people's religious beliefs, practices, values and attitudes. The interest was as much, if not more, in maintaining and developing the Church as an institution as in developing an understanding of what it was to be Catholic.[5] The surveys were premised on a logical, Tridentine way of being Catholic and an interest in establishing that logic. There was little interest in understanding the logic of how Catholics practised their religion. In other words, the practice of Church logic replaced the logic of Catholic practice. Finally, there was little evidence that the research was predicated on an interest in helping Irish people, particularly Catholics, to critically reflect on the power of the institutional Church, the hold it had in their lives, and in the way they saw, read and understood the world. It is perhaps no surprise that the findings of the surveys were primarily fed into the Church as institutional policy-making fodder – although the extent to which they actually helped formulate actual definite policies is questionable. Certainly, there is little evidence that the survey results were ever debated, discussed and used much by those committed to change in the Church.

What I am arguing here is that sociologists are often employed as tradespeople who work within a professional ethos of a value-free and objective social science. They investigate areas of social life and ask questions of people. However, the questions asked are proposed by institutions. The areas investigated and questions asked may not be in the interests of the members of these institutions. Effectively they are moulded into figures to meet institutional objectives. This raises questions not just about the belief in a disinterested or objective sociology, but about the need for sociologists to be continually critically reflexive about in whose interests and for what purpose they sell their labour. There are no easy answers to these questions. I may, on the one hand, believe in and value the need to produce a comprehensive, cohesive theory about social life and, on the other the need to produce objective, valid and reliable statements about the social world. But I have to realise that academics and intellectuals, despite their best intentions, always speak from a certain social position, and their speech always has necessary, if unintended social effects.

One solution to this problem is action-oriented research. Here the issue of who produces knowledge about whom, is not just problematised, but built into the research programme and objectives. There is a deliberate attempt to bridge the gap between the social position of the researcher and those who are being researched. If the researcher recognises and accepts the social divisions in the world, and believes that knowledge should be directly oriented toward enabling the dominated to reduce these divisions, then the task is to work with the dominated to help them produce an alternative, resistant, truth about themselves.

Action-oriented research is directed at the emancipation of the dominated. This means that it cannot be in a language that is external to them, which they cannot appropriate. In other words, sociological knowledge may be produced in the interests of understanding those who are dominated, but unless it can be understood by those about whom it is produced, it may have the unintended consequence of adding to, rather than subtracting from, their domination.

Action oriented research has been central to feminist and adult education research.[6] Based on the premise that no research is 'disinterested', the key objective of such research is to ensure that it helps empower or emancipate those being studied. This necessitates that the subjects of the research are not just involved, but have control over, the research process. Reinterpreting Paulo Freire, we could say that 'banking' research, that is research that colonises and incorporates people into the system, has to be replaced by emancipatory research which enables them to analyse and critically reflect about their world in their own words.

Banking research can, then, be seen as part of a system of symbolic domination that is based on people interpreting the issues and problems in their lives in an alien way, in the language, terms and conditions of outsiders, which may not be relevant to them, and have no meaning or importance for them.[7] As Lynch argues:

> By owning data about oppressed peoples, the 'experts' own part of them. The very owning and controlling of the stories of oppression adds further to the oppression as it means that there are now people who claim to know and understand you better than you understand yourself; there are experts there to interpret your world and speak on your behalf.[8]

If social scientific research is to avoid disenfranchising the marginalised and dispossessed, then it is obliged to have their interests at the forefront of any study. This means that there has to be a reciprocal relationship between the researcher and the researched. Those being researched have to have control of what is researched, how it is researched and, most important, over the report – how it is written and produced, and how it is disseminated and publicised.[9]

These issues came to the fore in a study of daytime adult education groups in which I was involved in the 1990s. The aim of the study was to identify and describe the different daytime groups that had developed around Ireland in the 1990s, to document the issues and problems which they faced, and to give recognition to the work and struggle of the groups. Not only was the study initiated and directed by members of the groups, but they had a veto on how the report was written.[10]

This raises fundamental questions about the independence of science and the scientist, and how scientific knowledge (truth) can be politically compromised. This was, in effect, central to the study concerned as during the research I realised that I wanted to explain the struggle of daytime groups in more sociological language. The compromise was that I wrote a more academic article explaining the daytime groups in terms of them resisting and challenging existing educational discourses and structures, and how each group was engaged in a specific site struggle for recognition and acceptance.[11]

It seems to me that action oriented research poses questions for the Church. It is not just a question of Catholics accessing knowledge and information about their Church. It also has to do with them producing their own knowledge and truth about the Church. But what does it mean to speak the truth about the Church? Is the emancipatory interest in liberating people from the Church, or from within the Church? Is the interest in liberating the Church from itself, and helping it to realise the emancipatory interests of its members?

Again, many questions without many answers. But, for me, any response, any attempt to deal with freedom and emancipation, has to start with the issue of power.

Power and Empowerment

One of the problems with the incorporation of the language and experience of the oppressed is that it can interfere with, if not undermine, a scientific knowledge and understanding of the way power operates. Freire, who decried teaching people to read their world in terms and concepts they could not understand, was equally adamant about the need for theory. *Pedagogy of the Oppressed* is a plea for emancipatory as opposed to banking education, but it is also a sociological explanation of how colonial power operates. Similarly, while abstract theory definitely got in the way, Marx fully intended his three volumes of *Das Kapital* to be read by working class people as an explanation of how they were exploited and impoverished.

While the prevalence of Marxism in sociology and adult education has receded in recent years, there has been an increase in interest in power. But the interest in macro, structural and historical explanations of power has been replaced by micro, hermeneutic, short-term explanations, and an obsession with a psychology of the self. Power has become conflated with empowerment, and empowerment has become conflated with self-discovery, expression, realisation, transformation and so forth. This form of popular psychology has seeped into such diverse fields as work, religion, community development and adult education.

Towards the end of the 1980s, managers and trainers began to talk about the empowerment of workers, even though it was often a synonym for self-supervision if not exploitation. In the religious field, it seems that many of the inner-worldly new religious movements, such as the Promise Keepers in the United States, revolve more around self-transformation than salvation. Empowerment has also crept into community development. As part of the wake for state socialism, people talked about the necessity for disadvantaged groups and communities to look after their own needs and interests. While this sometimes meant groups and communities being given free reign to spend state funding, it also meant greater voluntary effort and reliance on community generated resources. In the world of adult education, there has been a growing tendency, particularly in the United States, to talk about emancipatory education and transformative learning. This emphasised the search for an authentic, true, self. Once realised, this transformed self would then be able to engage in effective communication with others, thereby creating the conditions for social change.[12] Looking back at my own upbringing in a good Catholic home, school, community and society, I would say that while the

Church may have empowered Irish society, it achieved this through a process of self-denial rather than self-realisation.

Explaining Power

Empowerment is important as it emphasises the role of agency in social and personal transformation. But the proponents of empowerment are not so good at developing a macro, long-term, structural, relational understanding of power. One of the contributions that sociologists can make is to help people understand how they have been constituted, limited and controlled by structure and forces that pre-exist them. I believe that empowerment can only become emancipation when people understand how their sense of self is constituted by long-term processes of social change, by social structures and discourses, by habits of the heart and mind, by the positions they occupy, and the practices they embody in the different social fields in which they operate. Unless I understand these processes, forces and structures, unless I understand how they operate through me, the truth of who I am, how I came to be the way I am, and how I can transform my sense of self, will evade me.

Often a key ingredient in this endeavour is to try to clarify and elucidate existing theories and concepts of power by applying them to concrete social contexts. The problem with the approach to empowerment and emancipation described above is that they eschew the need for a theory of power. They do not, for example, provide an explanation of how social fields are structured, how power operates in our lives, how it is produced and reproduced, by whom it is exercised, the strategies and tactics by which it is exercised. When people talk of empowerment it was important to know if there is a distinction between economic, political, social and cultural forms of power? When people talk about transformative learning, the question is how can people transform themselves without transforming the social structures, the discourses and institutions within which they have been constituted as individuals? And, surely, if one is to transform these structures and institutions, one needs to know how they operate as mechanisms of organised power. To become empowered or emancipated it is necessary to know how power works, not in a universal abstract way, but in a concrete, empirical way. For this reason, I have tended to concentrate in my sociological work on how power operates in Irish society. My interest is in the present, specifically how Irish society and culture came to be the way there are today. My particular interest is explaining the shifts and changes in the discourses within which Irish people have sought to discover, reveal and announce the truth about themselves and, consequently, constitute and realise themselves as individuals, particularly, as ethical subjects.

Explaining the Power of the Catholic Church in Irish Society

It may seem contradictory, particularly to many committed members, to look at the Catholic Church in terms of power. How could a voluntary organisation, based on members developing collective meaning and identity through shared beliefs, values and practices, be analysed in terms similar to, for example, the state? But I was interested in how the Church came to have such an influence in the way Irish people saw, read and interpreted their world. In order to explain such an influence, it was necessary to examine the Church outside the structural-functional model that was dominant at the time. In some respects I was attempting to turn the way people have looked at the Church upside down while, at the same time, trying to avoid a crude Marxist explanation. Instead of looking at the Church as a voluntary organisation based on value-directed social action, I wanted to see what the Church would look like if it was analysed from a materialist perspective in which it was seen less as a voluntary and more as a coercive organisation. In this perspective, membership and participation would be seen as based less on value commitment and more as a strategic action directed towards material ends.[13]

As I said in the first edition of *Moral Monopoly*, this was not a complete picture of the Church, it was more an attempt to challenge the orthodox view.[14] But given the reaction to the book and, in general the inability to deal with dissident views, it seems to be that there is not just an orthodoxy within the Church, but a universe of undisputed views and opinions that are beyond discussion, what Bourdieu calls a doxa which may, in effect, be central to its symbolic domination.[15] But, for me, to understand how power operates in our lives, it is essential to know how symbolic domination is created and maintained. It is part of a commitment to search for the truth, part of my professional practice as a sociologist, to resist and challenge that which is deemed to be indisputable.

The argument I tried to develop in *Moral Monopoly* was that the dominance of the Catholic Church in the Irish religious field, and in many other social fields throughout the twentieth century, was based on it having developed a monopoly over how to be spiritual and, more importantly, moral. Specifically, I argued that attaining religious capital became central to attaining other forms of capital – economic, cultural, social, and political capital. It was particularly crucial to people to attaining symbolic capital. I argued that the institutional dominance of the Church throughout the twentieth century could be linked to the dependence by mothers on the Church for honour and respect. In other words, to understand how the Church developed such influence over the State, education, health, social welfare and the media, it was necessary to understand how, at a more material, instrumental, level, being Catholic was tied into a struggle for power.[16]

The power of the Catholic Church was, then, based on how through its dominance of key social fields, it was able to develop and maintain a Catholic habitus in Irish society; an almost automatic way of reading, understanding and interpreting the world in a way that was structured by Church teaching. What has changed in Ireland is that the practices that emerge from this Catholic habitus are no longer crucial to attaining the different forms of capital available in these social fields.

It may also be that in the religious field the Church is having less influence in the way people construct and act out their own ethical life projects. In some respects, Irish people could be said to be breaking free from the monopoly which the Church developed over morality. But, at the same time, there is plenty of evidence that Catholic tradition is a major source of spiritual fulfilment, compensation and consolation. What is not clear is to what extent Irish Catholics wish to be free, autonomous agents, creating their own morality and spirituality, or to what extent they want a more responsible role in the Church.

Irish Sexuality

To understand the power of the Catholic Church in Ireland, it is necessary to move away from churches, schools, and institutional buildings, and see the way Church teaching became inscribed in the hearts, minds and souls of Irish Catholics. Bishops and other Church leaders often seem annoyed that the media continually tar them with the same brush of sexuality, and give the Church little coverage or credence for the work it does in other areas of social life. And yet I would argue that most of those who have critically reflected on growing up in the Catholic Church in Ireland during the last half of the twentieth century would accept that they were well tarred with the sexual brush. But, as Foucault reminded us, it is too easy to say that we were sexually repressed by the Church. It is a bit more complicated.

One of the conclusions that I had reached was that while enforcing a strict sexual morality became central to Church teaching in the nineteenth century, and was in the institutional interests of the Church, it was also in the interests of an aspiring Catholic bourgeoisie to adapt such a morality. Indeed they adopted this rigorous sexual morality so well that they became world leaders in avoiding marriage (through postponing it to a late age, or not marrying at all) and confining sex to marriage.

However, once married the Irish had one of the highest levels of fertility in Western society. It seemed then, that one of the legacies of the Church's monopoly over morality was not so much that it repressed sex but, as Foucault argued, that it made sex such a problem, invested sex so heavily in Irish bodies, that being sexual, announcing sexuality, became a major source of guilt, shame, awkwardness and embarrassment.

During the last half of the twentieth century, it was no longer in the interests of the new urban bourgeoisie to be chaste, pious, humble and pure. They rejected the traditional Catholic morality within which their parents had realised themselves as ethical subjects. They adopted the liberal individualist ethic propagated by the media and the marketplace. Within a generation they began to ask why it was that they had been sexually repressed and, then, to blame the Church for their lack of confidence, happiness and personal fulfilment.[17] This was one of the foundations of the search for scapegoats and what can be seen as a witch hunt against the Church in the 1990s.

So why do I speak so loudly about sex today? Because it brings us back to the doxa which the Church developed not just within Irish society, but within the research agenda of Irish sociology. To raise sexuality as an important issue for sociological investigation back in the 1980s, was to resist and challenge the truth about sex and sexuality that had been developed by the Church. Of course, there were writers, and artists who had grasped the nettle of sexuality, but among professionals, academics and intellectuals there was a noted silence. And yet we had one of the most unique demographic patterns in Western society with high levels of bachelors and spinsters, people avoiding marriage until a late age, and then, those who did get married having one of the highest levels of marital fertility. Is it a coincidence that Irish sexuality has only been taken seriously by sociologists and historians in the last ten years? Or is it a legacy of Catholic Church thinking that these issues are not suitable for public debate and discussion, let alone for academic research. In other words, it is not just that power produces knowledge and truth, but that it produces an unquestioned orthodoxy or doxa the characteristic feature of which is that certain social questions and issues are not raised or perhaps even thought of.

It would be nice to think that the sociologist, by revealing some form of domination and repression, could feel that he has played some important role in emancipation. But of course what often happens is that one form of domination becomes replaced by another. To put it crudely, it seems to me that having kicked the Church and priest out the door of the Irish bedroom, the marketplace and the pornographer have sneaked in through the window. Indeed it may well be that the ethical demands of pursuing desire and being sexually alive and attractive, are just as demanding, if not more so, than being chaste and pure.[18]

But there is an important issue here which relates to the role of the sociologist in revealing the nature of domination and oppression, the structure of social life, and the way power operates. This can be done by revealing the nature of people's practices, beliefs and values. In this way, social surveys can provide the knowledge and information that can lead to good social policies. But it also seems to me that revealing how power works is not something that is easily or necessarily realised through survey research. This brings us more into the realm of general, abstract theory. Such theory, I believe, has a crucial role to play in helping people search for truth and freedom, and that is why intellectual and academic freedom, and the role of independent universities are so crucial in mature, democratic, civil societies.

This, in turn, raises one of the great paradoxes of contemporary society which is that most professional sociologists are employed by the state. But what is this huge amorphous institution which regulates and controls so much of social life. What is the nature of its power? How is it linked to other forms of power? There was a time during the last century when the Catholic Church had considerable power over the Irish state. But this has dwindled significantly. If there was a need to understand the power of the Church in social and cultural life, there is an even greater need to understand the power of the state.

The State

Irish sociologists have failed to keep an analytical eye on the state, the most powerful institution in society. This may be due to the demise of Marxist sociology – in which the capitalist state was always central – and the rise of postmodernism and the importance given to discourse.

Whatever the reason, the position of the state is under-theorised in Irish sociology. We talk about the important role of the state in the modernisation of Irish society, but we fail have failed to explain adequately the way the state increasingly accrues its power, the increasing powers of the police, the increasing juridification of social life, and the way the state has come to obtain such a dominant role in such diverse social fields as housing, social welfare, health, education, family, sport, the environment and so forth.[19]

An indication of the power of the state, is that when it comes to scandals and corruption, one arm of the state investigates the other. We are led to believe that corruption is something pertaining to individual politicians or civil servants. How many stories, court cases, and public tribunals of inquiry are necessary to realise that corruption in Irish political life has been, and may still be, endemic. In this regard, sociologists need to investigate what exactly is the relation between big business and the state. How is this powerful relation created and maintained? What is the level of trust in the state and its institutions? What is the legitimacy of the state? We may have kicked Marxism out of the academy, but we are still left with the task of analysing the capitalist state.

Moreover, although we may have rejected the traditional Marxist notion of ideological state apparatuses, we are still left with the task of analysing the way the state creates and maintains not just its symbolic domination of civil society, but insofar as it maintains a monopoly over producing the truth, its symbolic violence. What is important here, is the way it produces the truth about itself. On a daily basis, this is done through producing, managing and spinning the news. Part of this involves, what would sometimes appear as, a deliberate conflation of nation and state. At another level, there is a need to analyse how the language of the state, the way its reading and understanding of social life, has colonised the lifeworld and the different interest groups within civil society.[20]

We also need a more critically reflective analysis about the way the state produces the truth about itself and society in general. I am thinking here about the nature of tribunals and the ways laws are interpreted and enforced.[21] Maybe this brings us into the realm of the sociology of law, but it seems to me that there is something fundamentally different about the way the legal field operates, the way the truth about the state is produced in these Tribunals and, in contrast, the way the state produces the truth about individuals so readily and effectively in courts of law on a daily basis.

This brings me to my final issue about the state to which sociologists might pay more attention; who polices the police? Ever since the case of the Kerry babies, there has been a question mark about how the accountability of the police and finding out the truth about what they do.[22] It seems that we are still in a regime where, by and large, they investigate the truth about themselves. It still seems that people are confessing to crimes which evidence would suggest they did not commit, and that the police are prone to use excessive pressure when it is not necessary. But, again, what is of issue for sociologists, is the larger question of the state dominating social life and, when in question, producing the truth about itself.

The Media

The media have come to play a crucial role in Irish society and, unlike the state, have received considerable attention from sociologists.[23] However, the media are an amorphous institution and play a contradictory role in relation to challenging and resisting existing regimes of power. At the level of news and current affairs, the media have come to play an important role as the fourth estate, gatekeeper of civil society and main watchdog over the state. Over the last fifty years, the media have replaced the Catholic Church as being the primary institution which calls the state to task and demands that it give an account of itself. Politicians have moved from wondering about the reaction of Church and its bishops to being fearful of the media and its journalists, photographers, and commentators.[24] But at the same time, and through advertisements often within the same space and time, the media have become the main force propagating materialism, individualism, liberalism, and consumption. Irish people are now realising themselves as ethical subjects as much through messages from the media as from the Catholic Church.

It is in these circumstances that sociologists have a role to play in developing alternative and resistant truths about the media to those which the media produce about themselves. We need to go beyond the issue of state regulation, or the media regulating itself through some kind of Press Council, and ask bigger, broader, long-term questions about how the media have come to symbolically dominate social life. It used to be that the signs of the Church were everywhere in everyday social life in Ireland. Now the signs of the media are everywhere. It used to be that priests and bishops were the social conscience of Irish society, now it is a collection of talk-show hosts, pundits, columnists and commentators.

Social Conscience

Through revealing how power operates and making valid and reliable statements about the social world, sociologists can play an important role in resisting and challenging the truths produced within existing regimes of power. Through a rigorous dedication to the search for truth, sociologists can contribute to debate and discussion in the public sphere, to the development and maturation of civil society and, most of all, to preventing power and money colonising culture and society.[25] Sociologists have, then, a role to play in helping to reveal society to itself, and in doing so, keeping an eye on those who claim to be the watchdogs or social conscience of society. This raises a question which brings me closer to the theme of this book. Given that the Church has tended to see itself as the social conscience of Irish society, how does its role differ from that of sociology?[26]

Perhaps the most obvious difference is the basis from which the Church and sociologists speak. The Church speaks on the basis of revealed truths that have been theologically refined into doctrines over the past two millennia. Sociology, on the other hand, can be seen as a project of the Enlightenment, has put its eggs firmly in the basket of reason, and has only been around for the last couple of hundred years. It is the balancing of this division between faith, (ideological commitment, or hard core principles that are beyond question), and the force of reasoned argument, which contrasts the way the Church and sociologists try to fulfil their roles as social critics and commentators.

Secondly, whereas bishops and diocesan priests tend to speak for the Church as an institution, academic sociologists tend to speak more as individuals. This leads to an interesting contrast. One of the things that has prevented the Church, particularly the Diocesan Church, from fulfilling its role as the social conscience of Irish society is the demand that those who contribute to debate and discussion in the public sphere, particularly in the media, speak in a doctrinally orthodox manner. They speak as spokespersons. On the other hand, sociologists hardly ever speak with a collective voice. It is rare that the Sociological Association of Ireland speaks out about public issues. When it has, it has tended to be on general rather than specific issues, for example about the misuse of survey findings during the debate prior to the Divorce Referendum. Indeed, the Sociological Association of Ireland has probably only survived on the basis of an unwritten rule of agreeing not to disagree in public.

Thirdly, when spoke-persons for the Church speak out in public, it is generally immediately known where they are speaking from. We know the values, norms and beliefs to which they are committed. However, sociologists often hide their ideological commitments behind the veil of scientific expertise. Sociologists may aspire to and believe in objectivity and value neutrality, but they always speak from an ideologically committed position which may not be always announced or articulated. And while I believe that it is possible to make valid and reliable statements which might be deemed facts, I do not believe that facts speak for themselves or tell the truth. The truth about who we are and how we came to be the way we are is far more complicated than making verifiable empirical statements about the world.[27]

Conclusion

There is, then, an ambivalence at the heart of this paper and perhaps at the heart of sociology. On the one hand, finding out what people actually do, say, believe and value – as opposed to speculation or presumption – is important to the constitution and organisation of a mature democratic society and to the formulation of good social policies. On the other hand, the production of social facts will not change the material interests that those who are in positions of power have in maintaining those positions. Do we really need any more information about the nature of poverty, disadvantage and oppression before we do anything about it?

I have argued for the importance of revealing how power operates, particularly in relation to symbolic domination and violence. But we must also recognise that the theory that is used to reveal the doxa, can itself become an unquestioned ideological commitment. Like many others, sociologists tend to have a hard core faith which is rarely doubted.

I have not said much about Christian faith and where it fits in or does not fit into my work. And yet, this essay has been something of a confession and, as Foucault reminded us, the duty to know who we are, to speak truthfully, and to bear witness against ourselves publicly has been the defining practice of Christianity.[28] If we are to understand the uniqueness of the reality in which we move, if we are to surface and reveal that which is taken for granted, if we are to question that which is deemed to be beyond question, if we are to avoid the potential tyranny of doxa, then sociologists have to reflect critically and continually about their ideological commitments, their secular faith, the institutions which employ them, the position they hold in these institutions, and the ideal and material interests which channel their ideas down some tracks rather than others.

Notes

1. The author would like to thank Raphael Gallagher and Michel Peillon who read and commented on an earlier version of this chapter.
2. This raises what Bourdieu has referred to as the fallacy of scholasticism. At one level this revolves around the separation of the logic of sociology from the logic of everyday life. At another, more important level, it centres on how social scientific rationality, and to a certain extent reason itself, becomes part of symbolic domination. See Pierre Bourdieu, *Pascalian Meditations* (Cambridge, Polity Press, 2000), p. 83.
3. This is an adaptation of Habermas' argument about the links between knowledge and human interests. See Jürgen Habermas, *Knowledge and Human Interests* (London, Heinemann, 1972), esp. appendix, pp. 301-17.
4. This is an adaptation of Weber's definition of power. See Max Weber, *Economy and* Society, ed. G. Roth and C. Wittich (California, University of California Press, 1978), p. 53.
5. I am concerned here with the interest behind seeking the knowledge rather than the inherent problem in positivistic type research of reducing the complexity of people's lives to numbers and variables which lend themselves to statistical analyses. For a good overview – and potential solutions – of these issues, from a committed empiricist position, see Ray Pawson, *A Measure for Measures* (London, Routledge, 1989).
6. See, for example, K. Lynch, 'Equality Studies, the Academy and the Role of Research in Emancipatory Social Change', The *Economic and Social Review*, 30:1 (1999), pp. 41-69; and A. Byrne and R. Lentin (eds) *(Re)searching Women: Feminist Research Methodologies in the Social Sciences in Ireland* (Dublin, IPA, 2000).
7. See Paulo Freire, *Pedagogy of the Oppressed* (Harmondsworth, Penguin, 1972). I have here presented Freire's argument in Bourdiuean language. It seems to be there is a symbiosis in their concept of symbolic domination. See Pierre Bourdieu, *Language & Symbolic Domination* (Cambridge, Polity Press, 1991).
8. Lynch, 'Equality Studies', op. cit. p. 48. It is, of course, the problem of experts who speak on behalf of others, and the exclusion of those who cannot speak on their own behalf, which is not only a key issue in social research, but in the procedures of deliberative democracy. See Jürgen Habermas, *Between Facts and Norms* (Cambridge, Polity Press, 1996), p.

351. The problem, however, is that critical theorists end up theorising or speaking on behalf of oppressed groups rather than working to take away the barriers that prevent people from speaking for themselves. On this point, see M. Apple, 'Introduction' in P. Lather, *Getting Smart: Feminist Research and Pedagogy With/In the Postmodern* (London, Routledge, 1991).

9. Lynch argues that emancipatory research demands that theoretical construction takes place in language that is recognisable and meaningful across disparate communities, particularly the academic and the 'local' or dispossessed. See Lynch 'Equality Studies', op. cit. p. 58. However, while she recognises this as demanding, she does not provide any real solution to this problem of marrying what she recognises as 'different epistemological standpoints'. Bourdieu, who is adamant that the language and logic of sociology should never be confused with the language and logic of everyday life, is equally adamant about the need for the specialised, scientific language of sociology. See Bourdieu, *Pascallian Meditations*, p. 113. For a good overview of Bourdieu's position on this issue, Pierre Bourdieu and Loïc Wacquant, *An Invitation to Reflexive Sociology* (Cambridge, Polity Press, 1992), pp. 26-36.

10. Tom Inglis (with Kay Bailey and Christine Murray) *Liberating Learning: A Report on daytime education groups* (Dublin, AONTAS, 1993), pp. 3, 7.

11. T. Inglis, 'Women and the Struggle for Daytime Adult Education in Ireland', *Studies in the Education of Adults*, 26:1 (1994), pp. 50-66.

12. For a more detailed review of these issues, see T. Inglis, 'Empowerment and Emancipation' *Adult Education Quarterly*, 48:1 (1997), pp. 3-17.

13· This dichotomy was based on Alexander's theory of social action and social order. See Jeffrey Alexander, Theoretical Logic in Sociology, Vol. 1. *Positivism, Presuppositions and Current Controversies* (Berkeley, University of California Press, 1982), pp. 64-112.

14. Tom Inglis, *Moral Monopoly: The Catholic Church in Modern Irish Society* (Dublin, Gill and Macmillan, 1987), p. 7.

15. Pierre Bourdieu, *Outline of a Theory of Practice* (Cambridge, Cambridge University Press, 1977), pp. 167-71.

16. The analysis of Irish Catholicism in terms of fields, habitus and capitals is more developed in the second edition of *Moral Monopoly*. See Tom

Inglis, *Moral Monopoly: The Rise and Fall of the Catholic Church in Modern Ireland.* 2nd edn (Dublin, UCD Press, 1998).

17. See T. Inglis, 'Foucualt, Bourdieu and the Field of Irish Sexuality' *Irish Journal of Sociology,* 7 (1997) p. 14.

18. See, T. Inglis, 'From Sexual Repression to Liberation', in M. Peillon and E. Slater (eds) *Encounters with Modern Ireland* (Dublin, Institute of Public Administration, 1998), p. 104.

19. This interpretation of the state as a set of institutions, differs somewhat from that provided by Tovey and Share. They include discursive institutions such as the mass media. I am inclined to see the media and, for example, social welfare, as separate social fields with their own discourses, habituses and practices, albeit that the state is often the dominant player in these fields. See Hiliary Tovey and Perry Share, *A Sociology of Ireland* (Dublin, Gill and Macmillan, 2000), p. 76.

20. In general, the role of interest groups in Irish society and the greater influence of some more than others, needs to be investigated, see M. Peillon, 'Interest Groups and the State' in P. Clancy, S. Drudy, K. Lynch and L. O'Dowd (eds), *Irish Society: Sociological Perspectives* (Dublin, IPA, 1995), pp. 358-78. Why is it, for example, that small interest groups such as publicans have had such influence over the state?

21. For a good discussion of these issues, see M. Corcoran and A. White, 'Irish Democracy and the Tribunals of Inquiry', pp. 185-96 in *Memories of the Present: A Sociological Chronicle of the Ireland, 1997-1998* (Dublin, IPA, 2000).

22. See P. O'Mahony, 'The Kerry Babies Case: Towards a Social Psychological Analysis', *Irish Journal of Psychology,* 13:2 (1992), pp. 223-238.

23. See M. Kelly and B. Rolston, 'Broadcasting in Ireland – Issues of National Identity and Censorship' in P. Clancy, S. Drudy, K. Lynch and L. O'Dowd (eds), *Irish Society: Sociological Perspectives* (Dublin, IPA, 1995), pp. 563-92; M. Kelly and B. O'Connor (eds), *Media Audiences in Ireland: Power and Cultural Identity* (Dublin, University College Dublin Press, 1997).

24. This theme is developed more in, T. Inglis, 'Irish Civil Society: From Church to Media Domination' in T. Inglis, Z. Mach and R. Mazanek (eds), *Religion and Politics: East-West Contrasts from Contemporary Europe* (Dublin, University College Dublin Press, 2000), pp. 49-67.

25. Readers may realise that I have shifted back into Habermasian language here, see Jürgen Habermas, *The Theory of Communicative Action: Vol. 2,*

trans. T. McCarthy (Cambridge, Polity Press, 1987). However, it is possible to make a connection between Foucault and Habermas. Leaving aside his rejection of universals and humanism, and his apparent slide into relativism, Foucault's genealogical analysis of power can be seen as central to an analysis of what prevents the realisation of the unconditionality of ideal speech situations on which mutual understanding is premised, see M. Kelly, 'Foucault, Habermas and the Self-Reflexivity of Critique' in M. Kelly (ed.) *Critique and Power: Recasting the Foucault/Habermas Debate* (Cambridge, Mass., MIT Press, 1994), pp. 365-400 (pp. 388-9). In this sense, it could be said that through focusing on discourses, apparatuses of power, and the body, Foucault was able to locate the sources of the colonisation of the lifeworld and the distortion of everyday communicative practice, see Axel Honneth, *The Critique of Power: Reflective Stages in a Critical Social Theory* (Cambridge, Mass., MIT Press, 1991), esp. pp. 270-302. Although Bourdieu is also critical of Habermas's ideal model of communication, much of his Bourdieu's own work could be read as an analysis of what prevents ideal communication taking place, see Bourdieu, *Pascallian Meditations,* pp. 65, 122.

26. L. Ryan, 'Church and Politics: The Last Twenty-five years', *The Furrow,* 30:1 (1979), pp. 3-18.

27. There was, as Szakolczai points out, a fine but essential line for Max Weber between science and belief, values and facts. However, the task of the scholar is to avoid falling into the trap of, on the one hand, pure objectivity (positivism), and on the other of commitment to a secular faith such as Marxism. See Arpád Szakowlczai, *Max Weber and Michel Foucault: Parallel life-works* (London, Routledge, 1998), p. 148.

28. Besides having to accept dogma as true and to accept the decisions of certain authorities in matters of truth, Foucault claimed that every Christian has the duty to know who not just his faults and the temptations to which he has been exposed, but what is happening to him, and to announce these things to other people. See Michel Foucault, 'The Hermeneutics of the Self' in J. Carrette, *Religion and Culture by Michel Foucault* (Manchester, Manchester University Press, 1999), pp. 169-70.

Food and the Soul:
Some Thoughts on the Role
of Sociology in
Contemporary Ireland

PERRY SHARE

As an attempt to examine the specific connections between social sciences and ethics, this chapter introduces the topic of the sociology of food and outlines how it may connect with ethical issues on the one hand, and different 'styles' of sociology on the other. While the sociology of food is poorly developed in the Irish context there is now a considerable international literature that reflects the gamut of sociological perspectives, from functionalism to playful postmodernist critique. At the same time there are significant ethical issues generated by the key trends within the globalising food industries: these include questions of plenty versus want; social relationships of employment; the dangers of over-surveillance of the population; and fundamental questions over the nature of life itself as stimulated by research into genetically modified (GM) foodstuffs. There are strands of information about the social aspects of food in Ireland, including historical analysis based on readings of the Brehon laws, and histories of food production. There is also a considerable body of nutritional knowledge. A contemporary Irish sociology of food will inevitably respond to and build upon these strands, but will also need to examine its ethical standpoint, in relation to the key questions of food production and consumption that face our society.

Introduction

In this article my intention is to draw attention to an area of Irish culture that I think merits close study, the sociology of food, of eating, of diet and of the sets of beliefs and values that accompany and shape the human ingestion of nourishment.

If we consider culture in its broader anthropological sense as 'the way people do things around here' then food, of course, is an important component. Along with dress, religious belief, language and kinship it provides one of the key markers of cultural identity. Conversely, one of the aspects of multiculturalism that some find joyful, and others threatening, is the multiplicity of ways of eating that are opening up to us. Recently I was in the town of Kilkeel in County Down. While this is a community that goes to some lengths to remind you of its own particular cultural identity, I visited the local supermarket to stock up on cheap and excellent Italian food and wine, while dining on 'Indian' food from the local carry out – which also offered something called European food, and pizza!

The sociology of food is a topic that has been neglected amongst the variety of aspects of social life with which sociologists concern themselves. A brief scan of any sociology textbook suggests that food and eating are of little or no interest to sociologists, along with those other common, mundane and everyday activities such as sleeping, washing-up, gambling, going to religious services, hanging out the laundry, drinking in pubs, commuting to work, work itself, socialising with friends and watching television. The sorts of things that most of the people spend most of the time doing: our culture, if you like.

There are many theories as to why sociologists are unconcerned with such topics. One is that they are, as activities, in essence boring: which is why they have been similarly ignored by novelists, filmmakers, popular songwriters and visual artists. The ambitious sociologist wishing to catch the eye of a publisher, potential employer or media outlet may be better advised to delve into the complexities of crime and deviance, political corruption or complex theoretical exegesis than to produce a treatise on daily life on the DART.

Feminist sociologists have long drawn our attention to the fact that the most neglected areas of social life have been those associated with women: hence the failure to seriously address housework, caring labour, romance fiction or popular media. Food and its preparation have long been associated with women and this may have put off the male-dominated sociology profession.

There is also a strong argument that sociologists are most influenced by the interests of the state. Since its origins in political economy and social reform, sociology has responded to the state's need for information and explanation about key public issues of poverty, class conflict, societal management and ideological control: hence the enthusiasm for studies of class, power, ideology and deviance. Perhaps this helps to explain why sociologists have tended to be more interested in structures and attitudes than in action – why sociologists of religion have, for example, been more concerned with theoretical questions of secularisation, for example, than in everyday popular religious practices – a topic they have largely left to anthropologists. But it is imperative that sociologists reflect the realities of people's lives. The 'privatisation' of life is an undeniable phenomenon that requires of sociologists that they do pay more attention to the domestic and the everyday.

Finally, the somewhat ambiguous location of sociology on the boundaries between science and non-science may also hold a key. There has been a tendency for sociology to present itself as a 'serious' activity: perhaps in over-compensation for its sometimes less than convincing claims to be a 'real science' up there with the 'hard' disciplines of physics, philosophy and economics. Popular, perhaps feminised activities like food preparation, housework or childcare may have seemed far too 'soft' to merit serious inclusion. And what is more, they even hold out potentialities for emotional involvement and pleasure! Perhaps the fact that so many leading sociologists have been the offspring of Protestant ministers of religion may underpin the undenied asceticism of much of the discipline; a suspicion of mine that has yet to be explored.

Sociological Styles

The manner in which Irish sociology has been shaped by the desires
and dictates of church, state and the discipline itself are the topic of
the second chapter of *A Sociology of Ireland*. Central to the discussion
in that book is the characterisation of three styles of sociology. These
can be briefly described as the *managerial* approach, associated with
the legacy of Émile Durkheim and, to an extent, Max Weber. This had
as its end the more rational understanding of society, and as a
consequence, its improvement. Such an ideal can also be discerned in
the Fabian origins of much of British sociology. The second approach
is the *critical*, associated most strongly with the Marxist tradition. This
could take both rationalist and more utopian forms, but was also
concerned with the betterment of modern society, even to the extent
of overthrowing its systems and structures. Within this tradition we
can also locate a strong thread of feminist thought. Finally, the work
of Simmel suggests a third style: the playful or intellectual approach.
This type of sociology, probably the least revered in the broader
community, exudes a fascination with social life itself. It is not
primarily concerned with acting upon that society, rather to explore its
manifest contradictions, foibles and patterns.

I am going to make use of this broad typology to think about how
Irish sociology might begin to concern itself with questions of food,
diet and eating. I hope to stimulate some thought about why Irish
sociologists might enter this area of discourse, and what they might
have to offer. I hope to be able to touch on some as yet rather
unformed questions of ethics, values and belief that of necessity must
help to inform and shape any emergent analysis and debates. As will
become clear I will be doing this through the prism of my own beliefs
and desires in relation to food issues.

To return to the typology offered earlier. In *A Sociology of Ireland*,[1]
Hilary Tovey and myself argued strongly that for a variety of reasons
Irish sociology has located itself firmly within the 'managerial'
tradition of sociological enquiry. It has oriented itself fairly rigidly to
instrumental questions shaped by church and state and has, from that

point of view, generated much 'useful' knowledge. It is perhaps ironic that the very usefulness of such knowledge to the technocratic elite has led sociology to find a readier audience, and perhaps a greater influence, amongst policymakers and legislators than amongst the broader populace or within the wider culture. We remark, as have others, on the failure of Irish sociology to find inclusion within public debates about the nature of our rapidly changing society. The ground is constantly ceded to historians, economists, journalists, lawyers and, more recently, psychologists and psychotherapists.

We also pose the question what do Irish people want from sociology, and what do Irish sociologists want themselves from the discipline? The former question is a very difficult one to answer. While there is no lack of students wishing to study sociology within our universities and institutes of technology, we know little of their response to what they find. There are notoriously few mechanisms within our education systems for student feedback or even for effective choice within disciplines. In the language of communication studies, we know little about the 'uses and gratifications' that the public derive from sociology. In terms of the broader public, books written from a sociological perspective seldom make a publishing impact. Influential studies of modern Irish life are more likely to stem from the efforts of journalists such as Fintan O'Toole, Gene Kerrigan or Ann-Marie Hourihane or historians such as the ubiquitous J.J. Lee.

Sociologists themselves are perhaps, as we suggest in *A Sociology of Ireland*, now more interested in moving away from the managerial and even the critical approaches, and are increasingly drawn to the intellectual and playful. Again, it is hard to be sure about the reasons for this. It may well reflect the 'cultural turn' in the Western social sciences, where a disillusionment with science and empiricism has led sociologists to explore other models of discourse, not least literary criticism, anthropology and media studies. Or it may reflect something of the nature of Irish society, where economic 'success' has led to a shift away from the concerns of a 'modernising' economy to a 'postmodern' one based on information technology, tourism and entertainment, where the ephemeral is increasingly the valuable.

There are many that will lament the apparent neglect of a critical approach in such a turn. Marxists such as Kieran Allen[2] in Ireland and Boris Frankel[3] in Australia have been sceptical and indeed scathing about how sociologists and other social scientists appear to have been mesmerised by the fascinating baubles of global capitalism. To such writers postmodernism is little more than a fashionable withdrawal from the realities of continued repression and inequality. As such it meshes perfectly with the contours of the new capitalism, where image is the most valuable commodity in the marketplace, and the realities of production are hidden away, generally in a far off country that does not enjoy the luxury of continental linguistic theory.

But I would pose the question: can a 'playful' orientation to sociology be as 'useful' as a positivistic one – whether of the managerial or critical type? Is it now as valid to seek to analyse the appearances of contemporary culture as to seek out its underlying structures? I would argue that it is now equally important to do *both*: to recognise that appearance and structure are as one; that the surface and the real are inseparable. This of course is not a novel argument, and I have no desire to replay the debates around postmodernism at this point. What I will now move on to do is to perhaps use some of these ideas to suggest where a sociological analysis of food in Irish society might lead us.

What Sort of Questions Might We Ask About Food?

Having sketched out some sort of a framework for thinking about the uses and attractions of sociology, I would now like to consider some aspects of the sociological analysis of food, and how Irish sociologists might usefully, critically – or even playfully – address the topic.

It is not surprising that even a cursory sociological examination of the field reveals the possibility of great complexity. Topics for discussion range from the *systems* within which food commodities are produced, distributed and consumed; the *symbolic* meanings of food within families, communities, nations and the media; the connections between food and *social inequality*, the structure and meaning of *food events* ('meals' to you and me); the nature and shape of *food choice*; questions of *nutrition*, diet and health; the complexities of food, *gender* and *ethnicity* . . . the list is as broad as the discipline of sociology itself.

Perhaps we can start by emphasising that food raises important *ethical* questions. In Ireland we may need no longer to relate to starvation amongst our own populace, but our experience now of being a well-fed, indeed overfed, nation, raises its own issues. Thus for example, we may question the ethics of a system that transports food products half way around the world, to provide us with 'fresh' green beans in December, oblivious to the destructive effects of intercontinental air freight. Or a fast food system built upon the cheap labour of schoolchildren and the poor, and a supermarket system erected on the basis of zero-hour contracts and exploitative labour relations. Or, perhaps most fundamentally, we might ponder the implications of a meat-based diet that is dependent on the slaughter and sometimes the suffering of other species of sentient beings, or of a food system that is intent on inserting the genes of fish into tomatoes and rendering possible the oxymoron of 'fresh for longer'.

Contemporary Irish food systems mirror in many ways those of other Western economies. While a number of food systems intertwine and cross-cut at local, regional and national levels, the power of multinational retailers and distributors is increasingly significant. The activities of such corporations have long been exposed to critique from sociologists and other social scientists (for sociologists of food and agriculture the works of US sociologist Jim Hightower in the 1970s were particularly significant in the development of this critique). Until the eruption of food scares such as BSE, *e coli* 0157, and most recently foot and mouth disease, however, such critiques have found little broad acceptance. In many ways the sociological exposés of food systems are now starting to find a broader resonance in a society that is increasingly sceptical of globalisation: reflected in part by the success of popular books such as Naomi Klein's *No Logo*[4] and Eric Schlosser's *Fast Food Nation*.[5]

Food, after all, underpinned the earliest development of a global society: driving the migrations of early peoples and the explorations of sixteenth century explorers and colonisers. Writing in the 1980s, Australian writer Philip McMichael, and Canadian Harriet Friedmann, amongst others, described the emergence of successive international food regimes, based on the global exchange of commodities such as meat, grain and sugar. It was these global trade circuits that intimately tied the consumption of tea, jam and white bread in nineteenth century Ireland to the lives of plantation workers and farmers in India, Australia and the Caribbean. Now Ireland has a few minor multinationals of its own (Kerry Foods, IAWS, Fyffes) spanning the world and competing with the behemoths of ConAgra, Nestle and Cadbury-Schweppes.

But in whose interests are such developments? Two decades ago Hilary Tovey[6] called into question the transformation of Irish dairy co-ops into food corporations. Organisations that had been established to develop solidarity and welfare for Irish farmers now provide stock market gains and profits to non-rural 'dry' shareholders. It is arguable that Irish farmers have lost out in the development of the 'Irish' food industry. How does it favour the farmer in Dingle if Kerry becomes one of the world's largest producers of artificial flavours: no doubt to be produced in a factory off the New England Turnpike?

Schlosser, in his analysis of the American fast food industry, reveals that the welfare of farmers, workers and consumers is not at the head of the agenda for the giant food corporations. Similarly there is extensive evidence[7] that the global food system is posing an increasing threat to both the economies and the ecologies of the Republic of Ireland. It been alleged recently that the major food corporations are deliberately polluting the worlds agriculture with GM crops, so as to render it impossible to determine the purity of seeds. GM material is beginning to turn up in 'organic' produce. There are clearly major ethical questions here for all social scientists with an interest in food. Sociologists are increasingly interested in the question of *food choice*. Is this anything more than intellectual voyeurism – a desire to know what the people next door are having for their dinner? Or, more worryingly perhaps, could a social scientific interest in food and eating form the basis of an intensified monitoring and surveillance of the population: a desire to pry into people's everyday lives to ensure they are *doing the right thing*? Or, perhaps more promisingly, can it form the basis of a critique of existing food relationships: a way to challenge the power of the global food players?

Such has the interest in this topic been that the British Economic and Social Research Council sponsored a major seven-year interdisciplinary study of food choice, led by sociologist Anne Murcott and titled 'The Nation's Diet'. In a summary report of the findings,[8] food choice is reported to be of interest to: 'government departments, in sectors of the food industry, by professionals in health, in education and in catering, and many more'. Furthermore, it is 'a question that is self-evidently open to social scientific investigation'. It is also clear that the term 'food choice' itself is open to numerous interpretations and their consequent methodological imperatives.

Nutritionists also have an abiding interest in food choice. Increasingly they are moving away from crude and aggregated measurements of food consumption towards methodological approaches drawn from sociology and anthropology. Such methods include food consumption diaries, analysis of household purchases, food frequency questionnaires and in-depth interviews.[9] Not surprisingly they are finding that food choice is shaped in many ways by questions of age, gender, ethnicity and class. In itself this calls into question the biomedical basis of the nutritionist approach.

In Ireland there is a slowly increasing knowledge about the basic facts of food consumption. The Irish Universities Nutrition Alliance reported earlier this year on their *North/South Ireland Food Consumption Survey*. This indicated that in some respects the Irish diet had changed little since the nineteenth century, with the staples remaining potatoes, dairy products, bread and tea. But not surprisingly this basic menu was supplemented with a broad range of food items from bananas (consumed by 27 per cent of the population during the survey week) to yoghurt (eaten by just one person in six).[10] The survey also revealed that 4 out of 10 of the population are 'overweight', and that the prevalence of obesity has increased sharply since 1990, especially amongst men.

Once again, there are major ethical questions to be asked in relation to the food that people choose to eat. Do we have a right to dictate what people 'should' eat? After all there is a long tradition of telling people, usually the poor, how to conduct their lives. Sociologists have sometimes been colluders in this disempowering activity. In particular, is it ethical to focus on individual choice and behaviour when the 'choices' that people can make about what they eat are so powerfully shaped by the interests of the food corporations. As Schlosser shows in relation to fast food, the public had to be encouraged to embrace the hamburger as an ideal food; when chicken emerged as half as costly to produce, the Chicken McNugget was energetically promoted. If there was money it, the Nut McCutlet would no doubt occupy a prominent place in the fast food pantheon.

Food in Ireland

We know something of the history of Irish food, though there has yet to be a systematic and comprehensive history of the Irish diet. Historical sources include Kelly's fascinating analysis of the Irish diet, based on a close reading of early law texts;[11] the Brehon laws had much to say on the topics of agriculture, land, animals and the rights and obligations in relation to food and drink. Clarkson's[12] discussion of the modernisation of the Irish diet is particularly instructive on the changes wrought by the Famine and the subsequent incorporation of Irish agriculture into the global food system. Mahon's[13] popular history of Irish food tends to emphasise the bucolic aspects, in a manner reminiscent of the influential cookery books of Maura Laverty (*Full & Plenty*). Crawford's[14] historical analysis of food retailing provides a useful indication of how and when the infrastructure for the distribution of industrial food developed in this country.

A challenge for sociology is to link the disparate elements of food-related social activity in into broader conceptions of *food system*. Such an approach has the capacity to link practices in relation to food into broader questions. For example, a study of organic food has the capacity to connect with questions about food regulation, issues of risk and trust.[15] The study of GM food also connects with broad issues about the practice of science, the influence of global multinational corporations over our food, and broader ethical questions about 'nature' and the human manipulation of life.[16] Perhaps there are ethical questions about food here that will be the most crucial for the twenty-first century: involving as they do a genuinely fundamental change in the nature of what we put into our mouths and our bodies.

It is widely acknowledged that our contemporary food systems are dominated and shaped by giant multinational corporations. In *Fast Food Nation* Schlosser demonstrates how the American meat industry is controlled by a handful of firms, as is the french fry industry, the chicken industry and so on. It is likely that Ireland is moving along a similar trajectory, for example in the dairy, supermarket and alcoholic drinks sectors. It is arguable that such oligopolies and oligopsonies are unhealthy for the quality and diversity of our food and drink. Similarly they are not good for those that work in the food industry. Our highly concentrated meat industry is beginning to see an exploitation of cheap, non-unionised immigrant labour (for example from Latvia and Brazil) that mirrors that in the USA.

Drawing Threads and Charting Futures
How has 'the sociology of food' responded to such questions, and how might it link to our earlier discussion of approaches within Irish sociology? In a review of the field Beardsworth & Keil[17] point to the functionalist, structuralist and developmentalist approaches to food. In a later overview, Atkins and Bowler[18] add the semiological, feminist, post-structuralist and post-modern. Each now commands quite an extensive bibliography and an expanding literature of its own.

The functionalist analyses of food and eating are most usefully placed within the 'managerial' approach. The most commonly manifest version of this approach is in the language of nutrition. As a quasi-medical discourse nutrition has attracted a remarkably low level of critical attention. The ubiquitous food pyramid and the positive qualities of mono-unsaturated fats, dietary fibre and even antioxidants have entered the popular consciousness with little apparent resistance. When a particular food element is shown to be less (or more) beneficial than had been thought it is rare that the nutrition discourse itself is called into question. The Australian sociologist of nutrition, John Coveney,[19] has shown how what he calls the 'nutrition landscape' is quite uncannily reflected in what he terms the domestic 'homespace'. It is perhaps not for nothing that nutritionists' study of diet is often termed 'surveillance'.

Critical sociological approaches to food, not surprisingly, span a variety of positions. Drawing on Marxist theories of globalisation and commodity capitalism, food systems theorists such as McMichael and Marsden[20] posit international networks of surplus accumulation and exploitation driven by multinational corporations and their political allies. Translated to the local level, such critical analyses have the capacity to examine the connections between diet, inequality and, usually, health. Feminist approaches, not surprisingly, draw attention to gender inequalities in food provision, consumption and distribution, in particular within families and other domestic units. The critical approach would also embrace the many ecological analyses of food systems, such as the developing 'food miles' critique.[21]

The 'playful/intellectual' approach is heavily influenced by the structuralist and semiotic approaches of Lèvi-Strauss and Barthes. The latter's semiotic analyses of food, especially as found in his celebrated *Mythologies* have spawned many imitators, from systematic semiological analyses to weekend supplement journalism. The approach also underpins the work of the increasing number of sociologists that study food for its own sake, rather than to provide the sort of directly 'useful' knowledge offered by nutritionists. At its worst such an approach offers little more than an extension of the vast body of writing about food that ranges from recipe books to restaurant reviews. It provides little that is systematic or theoretically informed.

At its best this approach can open up useful debate, and provide valuable information on the ways that people think, talk and feel about food; how emotional and practical considerations can underpin food choice.

It would be easy – and indeed satisfying – to conclude that the ideal sociological analysis of food and eating would combine elements of all perspectives! This would possibly be to evade difficult ethical decisions. The field of study for an Irish sociology, or sociologies of food, remains untilled. Those that enter it may wish to determine priorities and to lead research in particular directions. They may need to choose between a managerial approach that seeks to join with the state – perhaps to reduce the increasing levels of obesity in Irish society, perhaps to better respond to anorexia or bulimia. But such an approach also risks an intervention into people's everyday lives that may increase the exercise of power over them. We have already seen insurance companies seeking to use the results of genetic testing in order to load premiums or deny coverage. Perhaps knowledge of people's dietary preferences could be put to similar ends.

Alternatively it could be argued that an Irish sociology of food must adopt a critical approach. The encroaching power of the food giants is as threatening here as it is elsewhere in the world. Increasingly the power to influence the production, distribution and retailing of Irish food will be ceded to the transnationals: from Tesco to Diageo, Unilever to Philip Morris. If the results are the same as elsewhere the process will see a transfer of power away from the consumer and the independent producer towards the corporation, and away from the local state to the multinational regulators such as the World Trade Organisation. A critical sociology, that exposes such processes, might just allow for some sort of public response.

But perhaps an intellectual or even 'playful' response is what is required. It may be that the most effective way for sociologists to confront the power of the food industries is to play them at their own promotional games: for example to celebrate the diversity of interpretations and uses that people bring to the consumption of food, as they do of all consumer goods. The consumer is not always a placid and gormless recipient of the products of the food industries. In the face of the omniscience of Guinness/Diageo they joyfully reject and deride the attempts to foist upon them Guinness Light or Breo. It is a remarkable feature that the Irish diet as described in the law texts of AD 8 is not remarkably different from that reported in the recent North/South consumption survey. Regardless of the massive changes that have taken place over the last 13 centuries, Irish people are still finding gustatory satisfaction in milk, grain, legumes and meat – with potatoes, sugar and tea the most additions. So it may be that sociologists should focus on an exploration of Irish people's general satisfaction and enjoyment of the food they now can obtain, for the cast majority, in ample proportions. It is a central part of or culture, and can be celebrated as such.

In conclusion, what I have tried to do in this paper is to introduce an area of Irish culture that I think merits close study. The options of how to carry forward such study are many. An important aspect will inevitably be the ethical aspect. While I claim no expertise at all in the matter of ethics, it is clear to me that we are at an important decision point – indeed a number of important points – in relation to how our food is produced, distributed and consumed. Not the least of these is the sort of tampering with life forms that is becoming an increasingly common part of the food industries. I have not dwelt on many other ethical and evaluative aspects in relation to food, such as global inequalities, the changes in our children's knowledge and understanding of food, nor the blurring of food and medicine through so-called 'functional foods' and 'nutriceuticals'. The topic is vast, but I have hoped to show that it is one that can and should be of abiding sociological interest.

Notes

1. H. Tovey, and P. Share, *A Sociology of Ireland* (Dublin, Gill & Macmillan, 2000).
2. K. Allen, *The Celtic Tiger* (London, Routledge, 2000).
3. B. Frankel, *From the Prophets Deserts Come* (Melbourne, Arena, 1992).
4. N. Klein, *No Logo* (London, Flamingo, 2000).
5. E. Schlosser, *Fast Food Nation: What the all-American meal is doing to the world* (London, Allen Lane/Penguin, 2001).
6. H. Tovey, 'Milking the farmer? Modernisation and marginalisation in Irish dairy farming' in M. Kelly *et al* (eds) *Power, Conflict and Inequality* (Dublin, Turoe, 1982).
7. H. Norberg-Hodge, T. Merrifield and S. Gorelick, *Bringing the Food Economy Home: The social, ecological and economic benefits of local food* (Dartington, International Society for Ecology and Culture/ISEC, 2000).
8. A. Murcott (ed.), *The Nation's Diet: The social science of food choice* (Harlow, Longman, 1998), p. 2.
9. G. Roos and R. Prättälä, *Disparities in Food Habit: review of research in 15 European countries* (Helsinki, National Public Health Institute, 1999), Appendix 9.
10. M. Kiely, *North/South Ireland Food Consumption Survey* (Dublin, Food Safety Promotion Board, 2001), pp. 16-17.
11. F. Kelly, *Early Irish Farming: A study based mainly on the law-texts of the 7th and 8th centuries AD* (Dublin, Dublin Institute of Advanced Studies, 1998).
12. L. Clarkson, 'The modernisation of the Irish diet, 1740-1920' in J. Davis (ed.), *Rural change in Ireland* (Belfast, Institute of Irish Studies, Queen's University Belfast, 1999).
13. B. Mahon, *Land of Milk and Honey: the story of traditional Irish food and drink* (Cork, Mercier, 1998).
14. E.M., Crawford, 'Food retailing, nutrition and health in Ireland, 1839-1989: one hundred and fifty years of eating' in A. den Hartog (ed.), *Food, Technology, Science and Marketing: European diet in the twentieth century* (East Lothian, Tuckwell, 1995.
15. P. Share, 'Trust me, I'm organic!' in M. Corcoran and M. Peillon (eds), *Ireland Unbound: A turn of the century chronicle* (Dublin, Institute of Public Administration, 2002).
16. G. Myerson, *Donna Haraway and GM foods* (Cambridge, Icon, 2000).

17. A. Beardsworth, and T. Keil, *Sociology on the Menu: An invitation to the study of food and society* (London, Routledge, 1997).

18. P. Atkins, and I. Bowler, *Food in Society: Economy, culture, geography* (London, Arnold, 2001).

19. J. Coveney, *Food, Morals and Meaning: The pleasures and anxiety of eating* (London, Routledge, 2000).

20. T. Marsden and Philip McMichael, 'Food matters and the matter of food: towards a new food governance?' *Sociologia Ruralis,* 40:1 (2000), pp. 20-29.

21. Norberg-Hodge *et al,* 2000.

Youth 2K:
The Multiple Worlds of
Young People

DAVID TUOHY

Youth 2K: Threat or Promise to a Religious Culture? *(Tuohy and Cairns) explored value formation among 17-24 year olds in Ireland, using an in-depth interview technique. A key focus of the study was on their religious values in the context of other values relating to home, school, work, peers and society in general.*

The study explored two forces on value formation: an external sociological force seen in current trends in youth culture and an internal psychological dynamic arising from the developmental needs of the young person. These forces interact in the worlds young people inhabit, giving rise to different dynamics in each world and a highly nuanced profile of the content of these worlds for individuals and groups. As young people move between their different worlds, the pattern of adaptation can give rise to problems of language and expression that present methodological issues for observers and interpreters. This paper explores some of the issues that arose in interpreting the interview data in the Youth 2K *study.*

Introduction

Youth 2K: Threat or Promise to a Religious Culture[1] was commissioned as a study of the religious sensibility and culture of young people. At the outset of the study, we were aware of a number of quantitative studies that measured young people's religious attitudes, values and practices. We were concerned that, in these studies, young people were asked to respond to items constructed from a set of adult concerns and perspectives on a relationship with God and affiliation to Church. Our concern centred on the possibility that young people's experience and worldview might be constructed within a different language and set of images than our adult ones. Young people are often well aware of the language of the older generation, but adults are frequently unaware of, or fail to understand the language being used by the young. In that context, asking direct questions from adult concerns may well extract reactions to the world of adults, but reveal little of the dynamics that give meaning to the lives of young people themselves. This concern gave rise to two decisions in the design of the study. Firstly, the study was conducted as a listening exercise, giving young people ample opportunity to reveal the dynamics of the formation of meaning in their lives. Secondly, the study focused on wider issues than a narrow definition of religious experience, exploring the meaning young people brought to many different aspects of their lives. In this paper, the focus is on three key issues for such research:

- The Complexity of Culture
- The Individual in Dialogue with Culture – the psychological dimension.
- The Problem of Language.

The Complexity of Culture
Schein defined culture as:

> A pattern of basic assumptions – invented, developed or discovered by a given group in learning to cope with problems of external adaptation and internal integration – that has worked well enough to be considered valid and, therefore, to be taught to new members as the correct way to perceive, think and feel in relation to those problems.[2]

By referring to a pattern of basic assumptions, Schein's definition emphasises the configurational and non-material nature of culture. Culture is not something a society has, but rather something it is. This makes its description all the more difficult. If culture is embedded in assumptions, then typically, those who have them are often not conscious of them, or their influence. Therefore, our understanding of cultural assumptions is inferred from other observations. The choice and quality of such observations determines the validity of the inferences.

Figure I   **Three levels at which culture is studied – the content of these levels and typical activity associated with the study.[3]**

Level	Content	Study Activity
Artefacts	Visible Rituals, Roles, Norms	Observe, Describe
Values	Images of the Desirable	Understand
Assumptions	Convictions	Empathise

Schein describes three levels at which culture can be studied – artefacts, values and assumptions. (Figure 1). Artefacts refer to the visible actions and rituals within a group. The study of artefacts describes what a group does, and how people behave in that group. There are no inferences as to why they behave in that way, or the meaning they give to that behaviour. Artefacts are easy to observe and measure. They can be described in terms of distribution and persistence over time. However, they are difficult to interpret. Artefacts can be used in the same way by different groups, but with very different meanings attached to their use. For instance, Mass attendance is measured as a cultural artefact. For some, Mass may be a ritual means of nurturing a particular experience of God and community, where that experience is the end to be achieved. For others, Mass attendance may be the central element in an individual's self-identity as a Church member. The same artefact gives rise to many different meanings.

Values can be defined as the images and conceptions of the desirable. They influence the selection of goals and the means to achieve them. Values may be implicit or explicit, normative or preferential and central or peripheral. Describing the values that underpin actions can be difficult, as there is often a tension that exists between the values espoused and the values that govern behaviour.

Assumptions refer to the network of ideas and convictions about the group, its purpose and how it should be organised. These enshrine assumptions about the relationship of the group to the environment and about human relationships within a group. They also encompass assumptions about human nature and activity, as well as assumptions about truth and time.

Studies on the religious values of young people frequently take on an evaluative dimension, where the study tries to assess how well young people have assimilated a particular religious perspective, or else it makes comparisons between different cohorts of young people as to their religious beliefs, where these cohorts represent different communities (e.g. countries) or different eras. Measurements are made in terms of the artefacts of the culture. The danger is that the culture is then seen as a product of these artefacts. The research issues focus on the reliability of the data – particularly how stable measurement scales are over time. The imagery of the research is taken more from the world of the physical sciences than from biology, where there is a process of continual adaptation. In ecological studies, the change of one artefact in an environment can often be compensated for by adaptation in another area. Therefore measuring the change in the chosen artefact may not give a full picture. What is needed in this latter scenario is a greater emphasis on validity, especially the construct validity of the instrument used.

To illustrate this phenomenon, we considered some tensions that exist in the world of religion. The history of the Church's self-understanding has been informed by changing emphases within the following perspectives: Redemption-Creation, Body-Soul, Law-Spirit, Church-Kingdom, Sacrament-Word, Transcendent-Immanent. Also,

Dulles[4] developed a number of different models of Church, each of which witnessed to a particular reality. To question young people about their assimilation on one particular model (e.g. institutional) and to find it on the wane, did not necessarily mean they had abandoned the notion of Church. It could mean that they were adopting a different model. Designing to encompass different possible shifts is what is meant by construct validity. I shall come back to some of these tensions in the section on language issues in the research.

Our awareness of different perspectives affected how we listened to the interviews. We sought to hear how young people dealt with the tensions generated by different perspectives. In terms of the design of the research, the implications of these different perspectives focused through two questions:

- Suppose we ask young people about religious values, and find they have none, do we want to know what values they have?
- Suppose we find that young people do not support 'old fashioned' religious values, do we want to find out what type of religious values they do support?

The first question broadened the context in which religious values might be found. The second looked at the breadth of the concept of religious values that might be explored with young people.

When the answers to both these questions was in the affirmative, we were not confident of designing an instrument that could positively explore the possible nuances of what the cultural assumptions might be. We were afraid of defining a religious culture in terms of a fixed product, reflecting only our own limited understanding. Therefore, we developed our design around an in-depth interview, with open-ended questions. We worked from the conviction that culture was a living thing, focused on the process of adaptation to internal and external issues. We defined religious sensibility as 'the way people are present to key events in their lives'. We saw the research as a process of prompting young people to talk about different areas in their lives, to identify the key issues and to describe how they were present to these issues, making sense of them and giving meaning to their existence.

The Psychological Dimension

The qualitative, in-depth interview sought to avoid treating culture, or religion, as a product. As we focused on process, we became aware of some key issues for the design of the research. At one level, it could be argued that culture, and religion, is *a priori* to those who are in dialogue with it. Therefore, young people seeking values and meaning are in a dialogue with something outside themselves, seeking both to integrate values and at the same time, generate new, personal, meaning. We began to address issues related to that process. Much of what we had read about cultural forces assumed that they worked over the whole population in the same way – that the effects of post-modernism are generic. Yet much of developmental psychology informs us of different concerns in particular age groups. Some of these concerns could be detected in comparative scores for different cohorts of young Irish people in the European Values Study (Table 1).

Table 1.   **A comparison of the average scores on five dimensions of religious practice for (a) two cohorts of 18-26 year olds (1981 and 1990) and (b) two longitudinal samples from the same age cohort (18-26 in 1981 and 27-35 in 1990) from the European Values Study.**

Values Dimension	18-26 yrs 1990		18-26 yrs 1981		27-35 yrs 1990
		(a)		(b)	
Traditional Values	4.7		4.7		5.0
Religiosity	2.9		3.0		3.4
Confidence in Church	1.1		1.1		1.4
Permissiveness	2.8		2.8		2.7
Civic Morality	7.6		7.6		8.4

Comparing the two surveys of 1981 and 1990, Hornesby-Smith and Whelan[5] found no overall change in the level of belief in traditional

Christian values or religiosity, a modest decline in confidence in the church, a significant increase in permissiveness and modest strengthening of civic morality among the 18-26 year old cohort. (Table 1, p. 197)

The authors found that age effects were more substantial than period effects. Younger respondents showed less likelihood of adhering to traditional beliefs and religiosity, had less confidence in the Church, a greater degree of permissiveness and lower standards of civic morality than older respondents. The authors found very similar patterns of change in all age cohorts between the two surveys. However, an examination of the youngest cohort (18-26 year olds) nine years later when they were 27-35, indicates major changes. The cohort showed an increasing acceptance of traditional beliefs and religiosity, a growing confidence in the Church, a lessening of permissiveness and a higher commitment to civic morality. We need to be careful in interpreting some of these figures, as the survey is not a true longitudinal sample, but takes two different samples from the one population in each of the periods. However, if the sample is representative of the age cohort in both periods, it poses questions as to the dynamics at work. For instance, one might wonder if the concerns of the 27-35 cohort (typically parenthood, etc.) were more congruent with the values being measured. The design of the interview sought to integrate possible psychological concerns of the stage that the interviewees had reached. For this, we relied on Erikson's[6] three tasks – identity, intimacy and ideology.

A second issue that concerned us was that young people might experience very different stimuli to growth in different areas of their lives. Fowler[8] described a third stage in faith development – synthetic-conventional – as characterised by the recognition of multiple worlds or frames of reference. As they learn to live in multiple worlds, young people try to synthesise information and values from each to form their own identity.[9] illustrated adolescent development as an interaction between three main worlds – family, peers and school (Figure 2, p. 199). In this context, a world is defined as having its own

Figure 2.   **The multiple worlds of adolescents, and the boundaries they negotiate.**[7]

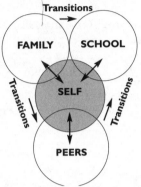

set of norms, attitudes, values, expectations and actions. In our study, we expanded the number of worlds facing a young person to include religion, home, education, work, peers, and environment. Some of these worlds were quite complex. For instance, the world of religion comprised a relationship with God, Church and morality. The world of peers included same-sex friendships, other-sex friendships, and included the new possibility of sexual relationships. This gave rise to a grid design for the interview analysis (Table 2, p. 200), where the analysis could deal with three different perspectives:

- Horizontal – how the three tasks were handled in each world.
- Vertical – the similarity of how any particular task was handled in the different worlds.
- Interaction of worlds – how young people dealt with the tensions that might exist between the different worlds.

When Erikson described the three tasks of early adulthood as developing personal identity, a capacity for intimacy and a lifestyle ideology, he saw the areas as independent, but linked. People can mature at different rates in each of the areas. Thus, one may have developed a strong personal identity while still remaining at an early stage of developing the capacity for intimacy. Head[10] described young people as entering into a moratorium on parts of their development. In the interviews, young people described different approaches to their relationship with God (intimacy), the Church (identity) and morality (ideology). This is an example of horizontal analysis in the world of religion.

Table 2   **Grid structure for analysis of interviews with individuals.**

World	Identity Tasks	Intimacy Tasks	Ideology Tasks
Religion			
Home			
Education			
Work			
Peers			
Environment			

Young people also experienced their different worlds in qualitatively distinct ways. For instance, the intimacy of home, and relationship with parents, gave way to the intimacy of friendship and relationships. No matter how positive family support had been, young people experienced the need to establish themselves as independent from the family. They were 'moving away' from the world of home, but they were 'moving to' the world of peers in a new and exciting way. Friendship, relationship and sexuality offered new forms of intimacy. Therefore, young people talked about the worlds in different ways. The vertical analysis showed similarities and dissimilarities between the worlds. For instance, there were strong parallels in the way many young people talked about developing a new relationship with God and developing a new relationship with their parents. There were also strong resonances in the imagery of good friendship based on discussion, self-revelation and shared values, and the aspirations young people had for Church. Such vertical analysis may give hints as how to develop successful intervention strategies in helping young people reflect on cultural issues.

A third focus of analysis looked at the way young people handled the different worlds. Successful negotiation of the different worlds was frequently difficult. The difficulties depended on how congruent different worlds were. For instance, male interviewees often reflected on having to learn a new language of communication when developing relationships with girls. They found the communication styles of the male peer groups incongruent with what was expected in a relationship. The pattern was less pronounced on the female side. On a more global level, the world of parents and the world of religion were often seen as congruent, but both were seen as incongruent with the world of peers. Hence, religion was described as 'OK for an older generation, but the world has moved on'. It was in this situation that young people developed strategies of adaptation. We notices three main strategies:

1. *Adopt one world and disparage others.* For instance, if home is the world devalued, the young person may begin to emotionally disengage, treating it as a 'bed and breakfast'. He or she enters into the world of peers in a wholehearted way, finding meaning and direction in the values and opinions of friends. However, some worlds are not easy to disengage from. Structural and socio-economic factors determine the possibility of disengaging from some worlds and entering into others (e.g. work), a factor that may cause complex intra-personal conflict.

2. *Take on different* persona *in each world.* In this mode, the young person tries to live different lives in each world they enter. They act out of different personalities depending on who they are with – friends, families, and work. This can often lead to elaborate patterns of deceit in relationships with parents when talking about peers, or in relationships with teachers regarding education. Conflicting loyalties lead to a fragmented identity.

3. *Integrating across worlds.* In this strategy, the young person tries to blend aspects of the different worlds without devaluing any one of them. They look for a level of consistency in themselves as they

negotiate the different worlds. This can be seen as a drive to authenticity.

The design complexities of such a multivariate analysis confirmed the decision to go for a qualitative analysis. As the main insights we sought were on means of making interventions into the religious culture of young people, we sacrificed the insight into the urgency or distribution of profiles, for a deeper understanding of particular profiles. Whereas a quantitative approach may have aggregated experiences and clusters of young people, the qualitative approach pushed us back to the level of the individual, where the developing profiles preserved the individuality of the interviewees. In effect, we were products of the post-modernist culture, avoiding an overarching meta-analysis

Language

Culture embraces a wide range of disparate elements (worlds) such as lifestyle, leisure, work, relationships and spirituality. Individuals engage with these elements at different levels of intensity. Some people are deeply immersed in parts of a culture. Others remain on the fringe. The intensity of involvement is mediated through language, and affirmed and reinforced through symbols, rituals and other socialising experiences. As we tried to understand the culture of the interviewees, we depended on their ability to describe their experiences, and also to interpret them. The quality of the interviews depended to some extent on the amount of reflection the young person had done on the subject of the interview and their ability to express themselves. For instance, we found that young people were much more fluent in the way they talked about relationships than when they came to talking about God, or religious experience. Three different sets of circumstances illustrate some of the problems with language.

Most of the young people we talked to claimed to believe in a personal god. Yet, when we discussed their images of god, we found a wide variety of understandings. They ranged from the God who sits in heaven, doing nothing, to a God who is actively involved in your life as a guide and friend. The following quotations focus on different images of a personal God.

He is there somewhere, but he doesn't do anything.

He's an old man, with loads of grey hair, sitting on this big gold chair.

(As a child) God was this important person. He's the one that controls your life. And now, when you are my age, you know that you are the one that controls your life. You do what you want to do. And like God is whoever you want it to be. You are your own God.

God is a kind of passive force, something that you can't really explain. Someone who doesn't interfere with everyday life. I think it important to believe in some kind of afterlife. It is good to make the effort to make people's lives better and not just to go for your own pleasure in this life.

I think he is just an ordinary simple person like ourselves, just kind of upstairs looking down and judging us and balancing the rights and wrongs.

When I think of God I think of someone like a father who absolutely idolises his children, who is there no matter what they do and is always there to listen and to guide and to comfort.

If you're ever in trouble, you can always turn to him.

He is a way of life for me.

At another level, we had interviewees who denied having an image of God or a relationship with him, but later in the interview, when we were discussing their hopes for the future, they expressed their confidence 'that things will work out for the best, because there is someone guiding the world'. For many other interviewees, this same belief would have been named as a deep personal belief in God. The issue here is the use of language. The meaning given to the image impacted on many other aspects of an interviewee's life, giving qualitatively different outcomes. In effect, there was wide variation not only in the distribution of responses in the sample, but also in the understanding of the question itself. In quantitative terms, standard error is not simply a product of sampling procedures, but also of the concepts used in measuring.

Interviewees also struggled to express their experiences. One question on the interview was 'Are you a religious person?' followed by 'What does this mean for you?' In responding to the question, interviewees revealed the complex structure of the concept of 'religious', admitting of relationship with God, Church and morality. Some young people responded: 'No. I don't go to mass. So, I'm not religious'. The response indicated that the interviewee had a norm of behaviour that created a boundary to the concept of religious. A similar norm was seen in response to how well they got on in school, where they focused on a particular level of academic achievement. Others responded to the question on being religious: 'Yes, I am. I don't go to Mass, or anything like that. But yes'. These interviewees were in the process of reframing what it meant to be religious. Some of them distinguished between 'being religious', which they saw in terms of institutional affiliation, and 'being spiritual', which they saw as experience and relationship based. When dealing with shifting paradigms, the danger is that we measure what people move away from, but we do not capture what they move towards or make assumptions that what they move towards is the opposite of what they move away from.

Concepts also took on different meanings in different worlds. One thing that struck us very forcibly in the section on relationships was the desire for honesty. Young people wanted to be honest with their partner, and the partner to be honest with them. They would often illustrate what this meant for them through anecdotes from their experience. They held high standards for themselves and for others. Some even applied this demand to institutions like the Church, and also to politicians. It seemed to be a pervasive and an underlying value in their lives. For some individuals, however, honesty was a factor only in their relationship with peers. When we examined their relationship with parents, and how they described their world of peers (socialising, drink, sexual activity) to their parents, we found high levels of deceit. Here, they took a more pragmatic view. Honesty was part of a relationship of equals, not a relationship with authority. I'm certain that such fragmented authenticity is not the preserve of the young, but the phenomenon of differentiated application of values is difficult to describe and measure.

The issues related above focus on the problem of language. This is particularly acute in developing quantitative measures. The application of qualitative measures does not necessarily solve the problem either, as we bring our own concepts to our listening. In the analysis of the interviews, our initial understanding of what was been said was often challenged. At times, our probes were not sufficient to guarantee confident and accurate interpretation.

Conclusion

In this paper, I have tried to outline some of the issues that guided the *Youth 2K* research. The dominant issue in the design of the research was the dynamics of the dialogue between faith and youth culture. Within that issue, there were major concerns about the validity of what we could discover. The first concern was with the complexity of what we were measuring. Any attempt to treat culture as a set of simple artefacts ran the danger of simplistic and misleading answers. Ignoring the developmental needs of young people might also give rise to misleading interpretations of their relationship with certain artefacts or values. We also needed to be aware of shifting language patterns, where young people ascribed different meanings to a concept than we did, or maybe even than a different sub-group within the youth group. The value of the approach we took is that it explores different types of assumptions within the culture. The drawback is the difficulty in making assertions about the distribution and intensity of such assumptions. This has major implications for planning priorities among those who work with young people.

Notes

1.   D. Tuohy and P. Cairns, *Youth 2K. Threat or Promise to a Religious Culture?* (Dublin, Marino Institute of Education, 2000).
2.   E. Schein, *Organizational Culture and Leadership* (San Francisco, Jossey-Bass, 1985), p. 3.
3.   Figure 1 based on Schein, *Organizational Culture and Leadership*.
4.   A. Dulles, *Models of the Church*, Dublin (Dublin, Gill and Macmillan, 1977).
5.   M.P. Hornsby-Smith and C.T. Whelan, 'Religious and Moral Values' in Whelan, C.T. (ed.) *Values and Social Change in Ireland* (Dublin, Gill and Macmillan, 1994).
6.   E. Erikson, *Identity, Youth and Crisis* (New York, Norton, 1968).
7.   Adapted from P. Phelan, A. Davidson, and H. Yu, *Adolescents' Worlds: negotiating Family, peers and school* (New York, Teachers College Columbia University Press, 1998).
8.   J. Fowler, *Stages of Faith: the psychology of human development and the quest for meaning* (San Francisco, Harper and Row, 1981)
9.   P. Phelan, A. Davidson, and H. Yu, *Adolescents' Worlds: negotiating Family, peers and school* (New York, Teachers College Columbia University Press, 1998).
10. J. Head, *Working with Adolescents. Constructing Identity*, London, Falmer Press, 1997

Indicators and Child Well-Being: Exploring Conceptual Measurement Issues[1]

ED CARROLL

Children do well when their families do well, and families do better when they live in supportive neighbourhoods. You can't serve a child without serving a family. We will not change the future of our most at-risk children until we change the present for their parents and communities.[2]

This paper will probe the manner in which the development of indicators can advance a comprehensive understanding of the child. Specifically I am concerned with examining a simple question: namely, how can child well-being be constituted and understood, especially when trying to embed it in the policy, systems and services of government? This is an ethical issue with far reaching implications for the provision of services for children. The context is the publication by the Irish Government of a National Children's Strategy and a proposal therein to produce a biannual State of the Child Report. Two key concepts – 'well-being' and 'indicators' – which are essential to the measuring exercise to capture the condition of children in Ireland – are outlined. The analysis will proceed to describe a model of valuable practice for catching the multiple horizons of a child's life: namely, a 'seven domains of living' approach. In addition, an application of the model to an Irish setting is mapped. This section of the research will draw extensively on national and international indicators particularly those used in the US.

Introduction

The 1998 United Nations Convention on the Rights of the Child (CRC) posits a view of the child that challenges the way policy, systems and services of government view children. Central to the task of the National Children's Strategy[3] (NCS) is the measurement of child well-being that advances a comprehensive understanding of the child. How can we help the exercise in its task of capturing the multiple horizons of the child? In what manner do child well-being indicators bring about a tangible improvement in the situation of children in Ireland? These questions are the point of departure for the exploration in this paper and expose the need for consideration of two essential topics: 'well-being' and 'indicators'. The analysis in this paper will then proceed to outline one recognised approach to capturing the multiple horizons of a child's life, and move on to propose its application to an Irish context.

Understanding Well-Being

Flowing from exceptance of the UN Convention on the Rights of the Child, the Irish government is called to make its distinctive commitment to enable all children find meaning and hope. In the broadest sense, the concept of 'well-being' is concerned with comprehending what it feels like to be alive, human and happy, from a child's perspective, in the family, community and society. The potential for such a wide canvass of enquiry means that the concept of child well-being can be difficult to delineate. It is dependent, among other things, on the specificity of the priorities set and the type of indicators developed to measure the child's quality of life against those preferences.

'Quality of life' is a theory closely aligned with the concept of 'well-being'. 'Quality of life' will most usefully encompass both the objective and subjective fields of human life. The objective field incorporates patterns and measures of well-being where there is a consensus on what constitutes significant components of better or worse life circumstances. Usually, objective measures specify the measurable conditions for well-being based on observable data (e.g.

the number of children who complete primary education each year). The subjective field incorporates measures of perceived well-being based on individual's personal values, views, perceptions, and experience of the circumstance of ones life. The subjective field comprises an approach that is focused on the person and elicits information based on what is said or done.[4] An example of a subjective approach exploring better or worse life satisfaction would be the significance of the home and school in the life of the child. For practical measurement purposes, the subjective field is based on an assumption that children or their proxy (e.g. mother) can be relied on to give a meaningful and comparable (across individuals and groups) answer to subjective questions such as: 'Are you happy'?

One of the challenges facing the National Children's Strategy (NCS) in its attempt to measure the quality of life of children in Ireland is the need to encompass both objective and subjective factors in *total well-being*. 'Total well-being' is a term that I would suggest to advocate going beyond traditional utilitarian measurements like economic well-being.[5] Broader notions of well-being refer to such things as personal and social values and preferences. While it is not feasible for this paper to define precisely 'well-being', it can be acknowledged that a flow of income or economic output is only one contributor to a child's quality of life. These objective fields must complement and interact with other important constituent factors (e.g. health, education and relationships). An example of a study that balanced objective and subjective factors is a report on the *Well-Being of Nations* produced by the Centre for Educational Research and Innovation (CERI).[6] This OECD study outlined four dimensions of a nations well-being: (1) sustainable consumption flow; (2) sustainable capital stock, i.e. physical, natural, human and social; (3) access to wealth, resources and income by different groups; (4) subjective well-being and life satisfaction.

Purpose of Child Well-Being Indicators
At this point, it is worth focusing on the specific issue of measurements used to assess well-being. Two questions are now posed for consideration:

(1) what exactly are indicators? (2) what purposes do they serve? A whole paper could be devoted to a consideration of the first question. I do not have space for such an analysis; however, it would be remiss of me if I do not make some brief observations about it. We cannot hope to survey in detail the complexity of the conceptual framework that would arise in any comprehensive answer to a definition of indicators.[7] However, I think there is need for clear distinctions in the terminology used. First, what drives the choice of an indicator, and judges it to be important, is usually defined in terms of *outcomes,* and should remain relatively stable over time. Stability is particularly important because it enables the indicator to show clear trends or differences that enable certain conclusions to be drawn. Second, an indicator must be distinguished from a *target* because it is much more freely adopted and does not have sensitivities to achievement that is entailed in the development of targets.[8] Third, child well-being indicators are not the same as *performance indicators. Performance indicators* are benchmarks set by a particular system or service to portrait a commitment to achieve something and on which its performance can be reasonably judged. Four, it is useful to distinguish clearly between inputs to well-being (e.g. material resources, education/learning, relationships and health are all inputs to well-being) and the arising indicators of well-being. Although inputs to well-being and indicators of well-being look outwardly rather similar, they are actually very different in practice.

The second question relates to the purpose of indicators and is a central concern of this paper. I would now like to draw out some of the insights emerging primarily from US studies. In the US there is an established research tradition on the role of indicators in monitoring child well-being. For example, Brown and Corbett,[9] propose five purposes namely to describe, monitor, set goals, give accountability and evaluate. Mark Friedman[10] of the US Fiscal Policy Studies Institute developed three key criteria for the choice of indicators. The three criteria are: (1) *communication power* whereby the indicator speaks to a broad range of audiences like policy makers, practitioners, providers of services, professional researchers and the person who is the subject of the investigation, i.e. the child; (2) *brokerage power* whereby the indicator tells something of central importance about the desired result; (3) and *data power* whereby the indicator can be tracked because high quality data is available on a periodic basis.

Kristin A. Moore[11] has developed a set of criteria for choosing indicators and I would like to select nine that I think are useful to the Irish context. These criteria are mainly concerned with the data and brokerage power of the exercise.

1. Indicators should assess child well-being across a broad survey of outcomes, behaviour and processes. In other words, indicators need to survey objective and subjective data. In addition, indicators should aspire to capture the life of the child, comprehensively, in a variety of fields or horizons, e.g. home, family, school, health, childcare, etc. The challenge here is whether comparable data is available in the chosen fields to make a realistic assessment. For instance, rates of disease and disability are different from educational attainment, and education is different from mental health yet they all measure an important aspect of children's well-being.

2. Indicators should be age appropriate and an effective system should also cover children of all ages, with age-appropriate measures from birth through adolescence or into adulthood. Ideally, we would like to be able to track children's development over the years of childhood, comparing pre-school children with school-age children, and with adolescents. This type of measurement is quite feasible for some highly concrete markers, such as mortality. In domains of living, such as behaviour, however, the relevant indicators will change as children get older. For example, markers of school readiness are needed for pre-school children, while indicators of delinquency, substance abuse, and other problem behaviours are appropriate for adolescents. In addition, it would also be useful to consider the inclusion of gender specific indicators.

3. Indicators should be clear and comprehensible. Indicators of children's well-being should assess depth, breadth, and duration. Measures of well-being at one point in time tell us something about the life of a child. Take for example the issue of child poverty. Children whose families are poor at the time of a survey are generally found to be disadvantaged compared to children whose families are not poor at that time. However, children whose families are found to be poor for multiple years are at even greater developmental risk. Thus indicators that take account of the depth or degree of poverty, the duration of poverty, and the breadth or accumulation of deprivation factors will be able to identify subgroups of children likely to face substantial developmental challenges.

4. Indicators should assess positive as well as negative aspects. There is a certain irony in applying the term 'well-being' to the current set of child and family indicators. Most indicators, in fact, measure just the opposite, assessing problems like infant mortality, substance abuse, violence, teen pregnancy, family poverty, and crime. It is unsettling that, at least statistically, we have a clearer sense of what we do not want for our children than what we do want. A significant challenge for all involved in measuring child well-being is to complement risk with meaningful growth and environmental factors.

5. Indicators should be collected now that anticipate the future and provide baseline data for subsequent trends. This means that indicators should be forward-looking. To the extent that we can anticipate future events and developments, we should be collecting indicators now that can provide baseline data for subsequent trends. For example, there is a reality emerging among children of refugees and immigrant workers that will need to be taken on board for the future.

6. Coverage of the population or event being monitored should be complete or very high, and data collection procedures should be

rigorous and consistent over time. This important criterion will ensure the robustness of the data collected.

7. Indicators should be developed not only at the national level but also at the local level. Indicators of child and family well-being should be geographically detailed. For instance, the transfer of authority evident in local development initiatives and regionalisation of children's policy underscores the need to track child and family well-being at least at the regional level and ideally at the local level as well.

8. The development of indicators is an expensive exercise and must be cost efficient. In Ireland, the setting of priorities by the Expert Committee to be established by the National Children's Office to develop a set of indicators is linked to achieving a better understanding of how children grow up. These priorities will determine to some extent the range of indicators chosen and will have cost implications that must be seen to give value for money.

9. Some indicators should allow us to track progress in meeting EU, UN, national, regional and local goals for child well-being. Indicators should reflect key social goals, thereby providing a useful tool for tracking progress in meeting international, national, and local priorities for children's well-being. This implies 'cross-fertilising' the work of researchers with the views of public officials, the general public, parents, and especially children about what are important and desirable outcomes for children.

The choice of indicators requires a careful examination of available data as well as inputs from various stakeholders.[12] For meaningful communication power, indicators require easy understanding by professional and non-professionals alike. For effective brokerage power it is important that indicators are balanced so that no single domain of children's lives dominates. For robust data power, indicators require reliable data, measured regularly so that they can be updated and show trends over time.

The goal of indicators is to make rights real for children.[13] This can by achieved by indicators capable of highlighting the impacts and implications of rapid economic and social changes on child well-being; monitor and report on any immediate deterioration, or on the lack of achievable improvements and suggest alternative strategies. Simply stated child well-being indicators describe the condition of children and monitor or track child outcomes. The selection of indicators is an imaginative and creative exercise that can highlight a positive construction of childhood in all its facets. Thus, indicators must be centred on the conditions of children and cannot be used primarily as a tool of endorsement for the practices of systems or services.

Seven-domain Approach to Measure Well-Being

Indicators of child well-being should encompass the depth and breadth of the child's life. The multiple horizons of a child's life can include family, peers, education, health, childcare, and so on. Each of these fields or domains of life, as they are sometimes called, provide an understanding of the situation of the child within that dimension. For example, Lawrence Abber described indicators within five domains of living relating to his work on child poverty. These are: (1) survival; (2) health and development; (3) status attainment; (4) beyond survival; (5) and children's rights.[14] Parker et al reviewed current academic and professional ideas to produce seven dimensions for assessing children's well being. These include: (1) health; (2) education; (3) family and social relationship; (4) emotional and behavioural development; (5) self care; (6) identity; and (7) social presentation.[15] A seven-domain approach based on work undertaken by Land and his colleagues[16] at Duke University is preferred here because it brings together a considerable expanse of research in the area and is not driven, specifically, by any domain, e.g. poverty, health, etc. He had another intention in choosing seven domains to which I will return at the end of the paper. These seven domains are taken from 'quality of life' research and include twenty eight measures (not included) distributed as follows:

Figure I   **Adapted from Land's Seven Domains of Living**[17]

Domains and Measures	Description of Domain
1. Material well-being supported by four measures	Assessment of the level of resources and wealth within the child's environment, i.e. parents, home and community. Concern with poverty and derivation levels experienced by the child, parents and community.
2. Social Relationships supported by two measures	Exploration of the social relationships experienced by the child in the family, school and among peers. Concern with the nature of relationships in fragile families and the level of involvement of parents with their childr`en.
3. Health supported by six measures	Examination of the general health status of children at key moments from birth through to adulthood.
4. Safety supported by six measures	Thematically related to the health field this domain assesses the child's security, i.e. as a victim and/or perpetrator. This domain also examines the emotional and behavioural development of the child.
5. Productive activity supported by two measures	This domain might more appropriately be named 'Learning Activity' since it is primarily concerned with the quality of a child's participation in pre-school, school, further education, trainin and to some extent work.
6. Place in Community supported by five measures	Assessment of the level of participation in the activities of one's local community. This domain can also relate to the level of achievement attained in schooling and access to employment.
7. Emotional and Spiritual Well-Being supported by three measures	This domain examines mental health, self-esteem, and spiritual well-being. It includes topics like belonging, suicide, and the place of belief.

Figure One is a representation of how the multiple dimensions of a child's life can be mapped using seven domains of experience. These domains have the capacity to identify those factors that contribute to and/or undermine the well-being of children. I would suggest that

Land's approach offers a model of valuable practice and is summative of the common key indicators that are being used in similar studies elsewhere.[18] The seven domains of living approach has been acknowledged as a major step forward in improving the stock of child well-being indicators and in stimulating important and influential research.[19] It includes commonly accepted domains like the child's social, psychological, physical and cognitive development and incorporates explicitly other significant fields, e.g. life in the community and spiritual well-being. The findings from the research have identified significant gaps in the current US indicator system for child well-being. Specifically, measurement and data in the areas of 'Social Relationships' and 'Emotional/Spiritual Well-Being' of children need to be intensified.

Mapping Child Well-Being

I would now like to consider each domain of living in terms of issues affecting children in Ireland and to suggest a list of indicators for each.[20] The purpose of this descriptive exercise is to contribute to an understanding of how indicators of child well-being can be visualised and to highlight those domains where there may be a deficiency of data to draw out any meaningful conclusion. Even where there is an absence of data in specific domains, this can highlight gaps that require new mechanisms for gathering data. At times, I will detail innovative themes and research that might usefully be addressed in future deliberation beyond this research.

1st Domain of Living: Material Well-Being

The 1998 United Nations Convention on the Rights of the Child (CRC) provides for the right to 'a standard of living adequate for physical, mental, spiritual, moral and social development' (Article 27).

The wording in the CRC suggests a relative measure, given that what is adequate for full participation in society will be higher where average incomes are higher. The concerns of the material well-being domain may include income, deprivation, exclusion, shelter, nourishment, and poverty. While Ireland has achieved sustained economic growth in recent years, it is clear that significant challenges exist to ensure the well-being of children in this domain. Early results of the *Living in Ireland Survey*, 1998, indicate that 12 per cent of children are living in 'consistent poverty'. The commitments made by the Irish government in ratifying the CRC must be seen to actualise the potential of children to realise their fundamental rights and to fully develop their human capacities in the decade ahead. For children living in poverty the reality is that their economic rights are being flagrantly violated.[21] What follows are examples of general indicators that have been selected from national and international studies that I have placed in this domain.

The US Government *Child Statistics Indicators*[22] mention five general indicators. These are: (1) child poverty and family income; (2) secure parental income; (3) housing problems; (4) food security; (5) access to health care.

Among the *Deprivation Poverty Indicators* developed by Townsend[23] and applied to families there are twenty indicators relevant to the material well-being domain. These include: (1) refrigerator; (2) washing machine; (3) telephone; (4) car; (5) colour TV; (6) a week's annual holiday away from home; (7) a dry damp-free dwelling; (8) heating for living rooms when it's cold; (9) central heating in the house; (10) an indoor toilet in the dwelling; (11) bath or shower; (12) a meal with meat, chicken or fish every second day; (13) a warm waterproof overcoat; (14) two pairs of strong shoes; (15) to be able to save; (16) a daily newspaper; (17) a roast meat joint or equivalent once a week; (18) a hobby or leisure activity; (19) new not secondhand clothes; (20) presents for friends or family once a year.

The ESRI *Living in Ireland* Survey[24] has incorporated eight indicators. These are: (1) a party on their birthday with friends; (2) school trips; (3) having friends home to play; (4) doing lessons, for example, music or dancing, or playing sports; (5) three meals a day; (6) pocket money; (7) toys such as dolls or models; (8) a bicycle or sport equipment.

The Index of Social Health[25] included the following six measurements: (1) child poverty; (2) average weekly earnings; (3) unemployment; (4) persons receiving social assistance; (5) gap between rich and poor; (6) access to affordable housing.

Finally, the Combat Poverty Agency publication *Child Poverty in Ireland*[26] suggested five indicators. These are: (1) child poverty income and deprivation; (2) unemployment among families; (3) families in receipt of social welfare assistance; (4) children's participation in the work force; (5) families in need of housing.

It is reasonable to assume that a major priority of the indicators that are set in Ireland will be to address issues of poverty and social exclusion. Therefore, I would like to make some brief remarks about the importance of this subject. In a new study for the *Children's Rights Alliance*, John Sweeney, argues that government can take steps that will be successful in combating child poverty.[27] Poverty indicators can be primarily placed within the material well-being domain although there is also a relationship within other domains. An example of the relationship, showing the multi-dimesional nature of poverty, is illustrated by the prevalence, among children whose families are on low incomes, of educational disadvantage.

There is a strong tradition of gathering poverty data focused on the position of parents and by implication on children. Nolan and Whelan[28] identified a number of starting points for the development of indicators that are pertinent to the material well-being domain. For instance a definition that poverty is exclusion from the life of society owing to lack of resources can lead to a set of objective indicators that attempt to identify an income line that distinguishes the poor from the non-poor. This is known as the income poverty line and enables measurement of how many households have incomes below that line. This set of approaches show an income – deprivation relationship. These indicators should cover both relative and absolute income poverty, and should cover lack of essential goods and services as well as money.[29] Another approach is to set out to measure poverty based on deprivation of things regarded by society as necessities, taking income and other resources into account. This approach concludes that poverty is characterised by both a low standard of consumption and a low level of income and that it is necessary to identify the poor by both a deprivation and an income criterion.

The setting of goals to tackle child poverty will seek to capture child poverty patterns and will focus on three broad areas. These include: (1) the labour market (increases in unemployment and reductions in low wages); (2) family structure (particularly lone parenthood); and (3) the structure of welfare supports. The main challenge ahead lies not simply in acknowledging the importance of all three but resolving questions of the relative importance and interaction of these different factors.[30]

2nd Domain of Living: Social Relationships

This domain attempts to capture the centrality of relationships or friendships to the development of a child. Specifically it concerns the relationship during infant years with the mother and father, the extended family and community. In later years the importance of peers and other significant adults comes into play. The CRC provides for 'the right to live with parents and to maintain contact if separate from one or both.' (Article 9). Shared activities are an important part of family life that supports children's well-being by offering the opportunity for friendship with parents and siblings. The division of domestic and childcare duties is a related factor with implications for the well-being of children. In contrast to the first domain there are constraints on the data available to measure relationships. This is partly explained by the weakness of subjective indicators that would be the main source of data for this area of life. Such indicators would be the result of assessments made in focus groups, case studies, clinical studies and sample surveys that cannot be replicated in studies that utilise objective data, e.g. teenage birth rates. Among the indicators that I have selected there is an absence of growth and developmental factors and a predominance of indirect indicators located within risk factors.

The US *Fragile Families and Child Well-Being Study*[31] highlights four subjective factors that relate to a specific theme. These are: (1) conditions and capabilities of new unmarried parents, especially fathers, e.g. how many of these men hold steady jobs and how many are potentially dangerous to the mother and children? (2) nature of the relationships in fragile families, e.g. how many couples are involved in stable, long-term relationships and how many fathers are involved with their children? (3) factors pushing new unmarried parents together and factors pulling them apart, e.g. how do labour markets, welfare, and child support public policies affect family formation? (4) the way in which children are faring in fragile families.

The Combat Poverty Agency (CPA) Literature Review of Child Well-Being[32] noted five general indicators and these include: (1) family structure; (2) relationship between separated parents; (3) presence of role model for child of single parent families; (4) length of active time spent between child and parent; (5) level of contact with peers

A local study undertaken by the Youth Initiative Project (YIP)[33] in Dundalk explored risk factors at the level of relationships. This study highlighted eleven locally relevant indicators. These include: (1) asssociation with at-risk peers; (2) serious breakdown in and isolation from relationship with peers; (3) withdrawal from group/club/team commitment; (4) physical violence from peers; (5) experience of bullying; (6) antagonism within community, e.g. punishment beatings; (7) adult relationships experienced as exploitative; (8) isolation from siblings; (9) sexual abuse; (10) weak affective ties; (11) long periods at home alone

An innovative theme warranting investigation in this domain is the relationship between children and their families. It is acknowledged in international research that creating opportunities for families rightly places the spotlight on the importance of supporting families in order to improve child outcomes. Simply stated, children do well when their families do well. To illustrate one aspect of this relationship I would like to refer to the US *Fragile Families and Child Well-being Study*. The study design set out to address a range of questions including how do children fare in fragile families and how is their well-being affected by parental capacities and relationships, and by public policies? Sara McLanahan, the main researcher associated with the work, was particularly interested in terms of the relationship with the father. How do unmarried parents see the role of fathers? She argues that until recently, most child development experts have taken a rather narrow view of the father-child relationship, treating fathers primarily as breadwinners and viewing their influence on children as indirect via the mother. She contends that emerging literature on married fathers questions this assumption and is beginning to identify the numerous ways in which fathers can be involved in child rearing: providing economic support, nurturing and caregiving, engaging in leisure and play activities, providing moral guidance and discipline, ensuring the safety of the child, and tying the child to the community.

The importance of the fathers role is supported by Carlson[34] who found (using US longitudinal data) that active involvement by biological fathers, including biological fathers not living with their children, in the lives of their children can have a range of favourable impacts on adolescent behavioural outcomes, including school attendance, over and above the effect of family structure.

3rd Domain of Living: Health Well-Being

The CRC provides for 'the right to the highest attainable standard of health, and to have access to health and medical care, with particular emphasis on primary health care' (Article 24). Ireland has the highest population of young people in the EU representing approximately 29 per cent of the population.[35] The predominance of children in our society presents a significant challenge to government to ensure that health standards are in line with those in other European countries.[36] Indicators of child health in Ireland show that, according to many measurements, the health of Irish children lags behind that of children in other jurisdictions.[37]

In 2001 the *Child Health Performance Indicators Group* reviewed and agreed seventy national performance indicators. While there is a significant difference between performance indicators and indicators of child well-being the exercise might usefully inform work in the health domain. Other studies that have listed general indicators include:

The US Kids Count Indicators highlighted seven that are health related. These include: (1) general health status; (2) activity limitation; (3) low birthweight; (4) child mortality; (5) childhood immunisations; (6) adolescent mortality; (7) adolescent infant mortality births.

An important UNICEF study[38] includes three indicators: (1) under-five and young persons' mortality; (2) death rate for five to fourteen year olds from road accidents; (3) suicide rate for fifteen to twenty-four year old males.

Combat Poverty Agency's (CPA) publication *Child Poverty in Ireland* noted five potential indicators. These are: (1) mortality rate for children under five (2) child suicide; (3) child pedestrian/bicycle deaths; (4) birth rate for teenagers; (5) children on hospital waiting lists.

US Government *Child Statistics* include six indicators. These are: (1) infant mortality rate; (2) low birth weight rate; (3) mortality rate ages one to nineteen; (4) rate of children with very good or excellent health (as reported by their parents); (5) rate of children with activity limitations (as reported by their parents); (6) rate of overweight children and adolescents ages six to seventeen.

CPA's *Literature Review of Child Well-Being* noted five related to infant well-being. These were: (1) perinatal factors: average/above average weight of child at birth; (2) mother not smoking during pregnancy; (3) receipt of high quality child care which allows for positive interaction between child and adult; (4) receipt of early education (5) receipt of maternal and paternal caregiving in first two years of the child's life.

The main themes within this domain include mortality, illness in childhood (morbidity), disability, and health service utilisation. Mortality is central in any appraisal of child well-being since there is an intrinsic importance attached to life itself and the fact that other 'capabilities' are contingent on being alive. Much illness in childhood and mortality is related to preventable causes such as injuries and poisonings, infectious diseases and certain congenital anomalies. There is an obvious overlap between health and safety/behaviour within the seven-domain approach to child well-being. This is evidenced by several topics like smoking, alcohol abuse, and drug-taking that are considered firstly in the context of the safety/behavioural domain although they are clearly within health related issues.

4th Domain of Living: Safety and Behavioural Well-being

The CRC provides for the right to be protected from all forms of physical or mental violence, injury or abuse, neglect or negligent treatment, maltreatment or exploitation (Article 19). This domain explores the impact of change and diversity on children. One of the practical consequences of change is the manner in which children seek to be more independent and in control of decisions that affect them. These new freedoms bring increased responsibilities for adults in ensuring that children are safe. Up to the age of fifteen, Irish children compare favourably to the average for children in other countries for many risk factors such as smoking and alcohol consumption, while for exercise Ireland has one of the largest participation rates. However, there is evidence of a poor pattern of behaviour among older Irish teenagers particularly in terms of access to illicit drugs and higher smoking prevalence among females. It is generally acknowledged that where patterns of acting are established in adolescence they generally continue into adult life.[39]

The information sources for this domain of life can include figures compiled as part of international and national surveys and through subjective studies where information is gathered directly or indirectly (by proxy) on the child.

The Youth Risk Behaviour Surveillance System (YRBSS) is a research tool developed in the United States by the National Centre for Chronic Diseases. Those behaviours surveyed include six topics and include: (1) tobacco use; (2) unhealthy dietary behaviours; (3)

inadequate physical activity; (4) alcohol and other drug use; (5) sexual behaviours that may result in HIV infection, other sexually transmitted diseases, and unintended pregnancies; (6) behaviours that may result in intentional injuries (violence and suicide) and unintentional injuries (motor vehicle crashes). The YRBSS has been in operation in the United States since the 1990s and has been adapted to monitor a wide range of groups and identify patterns and the effectiveness of programme interventions.

In addition, this domain of life in the US seeks to draw on a significant base within the US national data series relating to issues such as juvenile justice, child safety and behavioural patterns among children. It includes such themes as crime – children as victims and/or perpetrator

The Health Behaviour in School-aged Children (HBSC) survey involves collaboration of researchers from several countries, under the auspices of the World Health Organisation Regional Office for Europe and a team of professional researchers from Canada and the United States. Comprehensive surveys of eleven, thirteen, and fifteen year olds are carried out every four years in an increasing number of countries and are used to investigate health issues within and across participating countries. Students from all participating countries were asked the same questions about smoking, alcohol consumption and exercise. This allows extremely useful comparisons of important health behaviours to be made between Irish children and their international counterparts.[40]

Finally, in 1998 the Health Promotion Unit in the Department of Health and Children as part of the World Health Organisation Survey conducted *The National Health & Lifestyles Surveys* (NHLS), which was completed in 1999, and this report has established Irish national health benchmarks. Among the measures used by the NHLS were: (1) general health; (2) smoking; (3) alcohol; (4) food and nutrition; (5) exercise; (6) accidents across the entire population.

5th Domain of Living: Productivity Well-Being

Although I would prefer to rename this domain of living as 'Learning Activities', the focus of this field is education, training and work. The choice of the word, 'productive', arises from the assumption that the primary productive activity of children is related to learning within pre-school, school or college. This understanding is influenced by the fact that in the EU there has been an instrumental view of the contribution of learning as largely a matter of having income and employment outcomes. However, education has many effects beyond that of increasing material living standards. These effects include the enrichment of a child's life in various ways, giving him or her the capability to achieve a wider set of independent living skills. The CRC provides for the right to education, and to the development of the child's abilities to their fullest potential (Articles 28 and 29). Furthermore, it underlines that countries should achieve educational rights 'on the basis of equal opportunity'. There are three challenges arising here that I would like to highlight.

First, the Irish school system provides a formal education for all children. The importance of the family and community in the education of the child is receiving greater recognition, but more needs to be done to strengthen the links between the family, community, and school. Second, in contemporary Ireland the requirement for entry to third-level higher education has been calculated by the points system. The points system uses results and selects people for progression towards third level courses. This system is probably the decisive agency in determining a child's economic future yet participation by lower socio-economic groups is hugely problematic.[41] Third, the importance of work for children is also significant area for investigation in this domain. The workforce includes 16 per cent of children in the fifteen to seventeen years age bracket. Almost 31 per cent of these young people undertake work on a full-time basis. While these children enjoy a number of additional protections under employment legislation, this level of work poses concerns for their educational attainment.[42]

There are various studies that list important indicators related to this domain. The US Government *Child Statistics* describes five indicators. These are: (1) percentage of children ages three to five who are read to every day by a family member; (2) percentage of children ages three to four who are enrolled in pre-school; (3) percentage of young adults ages eighteen to twenty-four who have completed High School; (4) percentage of young adults sixteen to eighteen who are neither in school nor working; (5) percentage of high school graduates ages twenty-five to twenty-nine who have completed a certificate, diploma or bachelor's award.

Among the US Kids Count Indicator list there are five indicators related to this domain. These include: (1) family reading to young children; (2) early childhood education; (3) mathematics and reading achievement upon high school completion; (4) youth neither enrolled in school nor working; (5) higher education enrollment

The CPA *Child Poverty in Ireland Report* marks out five areas for consideration. These are: (1) attendance at pre-school; (2) child literacy; (3) participation in education at aged sixteen; (4) non attendance at school (including children who are excluded); (5) children with disabilities attending mainstream education.

In a paper[43] provided by Guy Palmer, New Policy institute, in the context of the National Anti-Poverty Review six indicators related to the theme of children and employment were outlined. These include: (1) children in workless households; (2) children in low income households; (3) number of young adults unemployed; (4) number of young adults inactive; (5) number of young adults without a basic qualification.

Of particular interest is an approach highlighted within the CPA *Literature Review of Child Well-Being.* This noted five indicators focusing on the role and capacity of the school. These are: (1) ability of the school to address particular needs of the pupil; (2) parental involvement in school; (3) ability of the school to deal with disruptive pupils without excluding them; (4) pupil participation in running of the school; (5) adoption by the school of a holistic approach regarding education.

The importance of meaningful engagement with school can have direct effects on the level of the child's performance in school and reduce risk exposure. In addition, extracurricular activities has been linked to improved academic performance, reduced rates of early dropout and criminal arrest, and lower risk of school-age motherhood.[44] Thus, the domain of living related to education, training and work encompasses hugely significant and expansive aspects of the life of a child that need to be captured.

6th Domain of Living: Place in the Community Well-Being

A key to child well-being is the creation of supportive environments. Beyond the family the community has the potential to contribute to child well-being in a significant way. It has long been an insight of youth and community development work that we will not change the future of our most at-risk children until we change the present for their parents and communities. The increasing emphasis placed on the role of community also owes much to the growing popularity of the idea of social capital. Social capital[45] is a concept that tries to capture the significance of community, placing it at the centre of policy, systems and services. Strong communities sharing similar needs can be a special resource for children, supporting and nurturing the child, and in some cases ameliorating difficult family and social circumstances. The types of nurtured support can range from the reciprocal, material and emotional help between neighbours to more formalised interventions provided by the community for the community.[46] The vision behind strengthening the child's neighbourhood is that strong communities can offer education, a sense of community, social networks, accessible services and supports and economic opportunities.[47]

This domain has characteristics similar to the 'Social Relationships' domain because of its reliance on subjective data. Therefore there is an absence of data available for this domain and few indicators available for its measurement. The CPA *Literature Review of Child Well-Being* captured five indicators that can be placed in this domain of living. These are: (1) availability of quality play space and a clean environment; (2) access to preferred leisure/play areas; (3) proximity of community resources to the family home; (4) level of geographic mobility of child; (5) level of social capital within community

A Hawaii KIDS COUNT publication included a whole chapter on 'social conditions and community engagement.'[48] Among the descriptors used for the collection of data were: (1) the percentage of adults who feel they can rely on another person in their community for help; (2) the number of times per week children are in contact with an extended member of the family.

The National Children's Strategy signified the value of the community in the life of a child and set an objective that children will benefit from and contribute to vibrant local communities.[49] One of the insights that came from NCS consultation with children was how children valued the people in their neighbourhood. The implementation of this objective has the potential to realise the idea of social capital in action, i.e. a true appreciation of the role played by the community in child well being.

7th Domain of Living: Emotional And Spiritual Well-being

Child well-being is also captured by the manner in which children describe themselves. While Irish children have reported that they can feel low during the week, overall they are satisfied with their lives.[50] Emotional development includes a child's perception of oneself, the ability to understand the emotions of other people, and the ability to interpret and express ones own feelings. In addition, many studies have suggested, children are strongly affected by their parent's mental health. Addressing parent's psychological problems may have benefits for children, as may interventions that jointly address parent and child problems, such as depression.

In the NSAF a measure of poor emotional well-being was derived from a series of questions. Parents were asked to report the extent to which, in the past month, their children could not concentrate or pay attention for long, or were unhappy, sad, or depressed. A second question enquired, how often during the past month their children felt worthless or inferior, were nervous, highly strung, or tense. A third question directed at parents of twelve to seventeen-year-olds asked, how often during the past month their children had trouble sleeping, lied or cheated, or did poorly at schoolwork?[51]

One of the interesting issues raised by children in the NCS consultation process was the value of the child's experience of spirituality. It has been acknowledged that spirituality presents government with a problem in knowing how to respond appropriately to it.[52] The CRC provides for the 'right to freedom of thought, conscience and religion' (Article 14). The religious values of the child in the context of other values relating to home, school, work, peers and society in general has been the subject of recent study undertaken in Ireland.[53] Youth 2K was commissioned as a study of the religious sensibility and culture of young people. The concern of the study was on the possibility that young people's experience and worldview might be constructed within a different language and set of images than adult ones. The study was designed as a listening exercise, giving the child many opportunities to reveal the dynamics of the formation of meaning in their lives. In addition, the study focused on the wider issues than a narrow definition of religious experience (e.g. attendance at religious practices), exploring the meaning the child brought to many different aspects of their lives.[54]

Among the quantitative studies measuring the child's religious attitudes, values and practices are the following:

The US Child Statistics contains two indicator descriptors that can be located in this domain. These are: (1) rate of weekly religious attendance, Grade 12; (2) percentage who report religion as being very important, Grade 12.

The International Study Survey Programme (ISSP) was convened in 1984 by four survey centres. Its theme is to survey the religious attitudes and values of people including children.[55] They agreed that they would develop a fifteen-minute questionnaire. Each country committed itself to a representative probability sample of at least a thousand respondents. The Social Science Research Centre of University College Dublin joined the project and the ESRI has collated the data for Ireland. There are now survey centres for thirty seven nations, which participate in this study. Among the indicators used by the ISSP programme there is six of interest to a notion of spiritual well-being. These include: (1) religious attitudes and behaviours; (2) religious imagination in Ireland; (3) belief in God; (4) belief in life after death; (5) weekly mass; and (6) church activities.

In his recent study, Richard Kearney adverts to the fact that in an UNESCO questionnaire, distributed some years ago to leading thinkers, in which there was a question: what was the most important issue of our new millennium; the majority replied: religion.[56] This consideration of the spiritual well-being is quite appropriately among the 'last things' that this mapping exercise explores.

Issues Arising and Key Points

I would contend that a seven-domain approach differentiates in a rudimentary manner how the depth and breadth of the child's life can be encompassed. Essentially the mapping exercise must always aspire to combine and delicately balance a consideration of environmental, growth and risk factors impinging on the child. Earlier in the paper, I noted that Land's seven-domain approach had another purpose. It is appropriate to make some brief observations about this purpose because it illustrates quite well two technical limitations that require further research. These are: the comparability of indicators and the problem of aggregation. The goal of the seven-domain study was to create a single index of child well-being that would enable the comparability of indicators within and across the domains. In the US there are a considerable number of indicators of well-being available from the federal statistical system that relate how children are doing in particular aspects of their lives. But there are no generally accepted measures to tell us how they are doing overall. Furthermore those studies that do measure the well-being of children rarely use similar methods. As result, comparing outcomes across domains presents a significant challenge.

Land is developing the index in much the same way economists developed the Consumer Price Index, by grouping like measures together into broad domains of well-being, then combining the domains into a single index. The resulting index allows the tracking of overall well-being in the US on an annual basis from 1985 to the present. Multiple versions of the index, as well as various domain-specific indices, have been tested to create the most robust measure possible, one that is not too heavily affected by a single domain, age group, or outcome. In his work Land acknowledged that several of the domains are inadequately represented in the index due to a lack of available information. The domain-specific indices are more sound measures of particular elements of child well-being than the overall index. However, the problem of aggregation comes to the fore when dealing with subjective indicators predominant throughout the mapping exercise. The problem with any non-monetary variable is that you have no way of adding the parts up except by ascribing arbitrary weights to each component. Arguably, it is better to do it this way than simply ignore everything except some narrow measure based on income or consumption goods.

A broader issue arising from this paper concerns the way in which indicators of child well-being can achieve a tangible improvement in the situation of children and by association implement our obligations under CRC. In Ireland we have still to find a holistic way of capturing the life and condition of children. The measurement exercise implied by the development of indicators is an important instrument to ensure that children are empowered by all policy, systems and services to grow and develop to their full capacity. It is clearly one of the values of an instrument like the CRC that it can be used pragmatically to call government to account. However, beyond the achievement of good averages and a high rate of progress, there are other instruments required to ensure children's rights. I would suggest that there is something more important at stake here that always needs to be kept in focus. It relates to the nature of the relationship and connection between the CRC and the measurement exercise of child well-being. Essentially the CRC is founded on human rights that stand for clear values and principles that effect change by internalising a radical shift in the culture of State provision for children. Indicators of child well-being are scientific constructions that have a vital role to play in this task but can never guarantee the type of transformation required by the CRC. They are simply not of the same order and as an exercise well-being indicators must always be scrutinised on how well they contribute to promoting a new ethical attitude towards children.

In conclusion, this paper has tried to probe how best to advance a comprehensive understanding of the child. It has done this in a theoretical and practical way. At a theoretical level it has focused on child well-being indicators. The paper highlighted that the terms 'well-being' (especially its affinity with the notion of 'quality of life'), and 'indicators' were not easy to define precisely. Instead the analysis had to be more sober in its approach, seeking simply to characterise each. In relation to 'well-being' the paper argued that a complementary range of objective and subjective measurements be maintained. This means that any enquiry into the status of children in Ireland is required to move beyond traditional utilitarian measurements and include broader notions referring to personal and social values and preferences. The analysis of the paper also contended that the term 'indicators' has often been used imprecisely referring at once to inputs, targets and performance measurements. It was recommended that further research be undertaken into a conceptual framework for child well-being specifically distinguishing between inputs to well-being and indicators. The critique of the paper focused on the purpose of indicators advocating three requirements in the selection process. The three requirements of indicators include: (1) ease of understanding by professional and non-professionals alike; (2) balance so that no single domain of children's lives dominates; (3) reliable data, measured regularly so that they can be updated and show trends over time.

Notes

1. This article formed part of a larger publication entitled *The Well-Being of Children* (2002), which was prepared for the Irish Youth Foundation. It is reproduced with the kind permission of the Irish Youth Foundation.

2. AEC Annual Kids Count Survey (Washington, AEC Foundation, 2001).

3. Department of Health and Children *The National Children's Strategy – Our Children Their Lives* (Dublin, Stationary Office, 2000).

4. Land locates the subject approach in the methodological detail adopted by F. M. Andrews, and S.B.Withey, *Social Indicators of Well-Being: American's Perception of Quality of Life* (New York, Plenum Press, 1976). See also A.Campbell, P. Converse, and W.L.Rogers, *The Quality of American Life* (New York, Russell Sage Foundation, 1976).

5. During an informal meeting, Peter Evans, OECD Centre for Educational Research and Innovation, suggested that there is now a greater acknowledgment that traditional utilitarian indicators have been wholly inadequate and that the capability approach developed by Amartya Sen works out of a different analytical model. Sen's capability approach has equivalencies with a rights approach in that it seeks to measure the efforts undertaken to ensure that people have equal access to basic capabilities. These include: the ability to be healthy; well-fed; housed; integrated into the community; participate in community and public life; and enjoy social bases of self-respect.

6. Centre for Educational Research and Innovation, *The Well-Being of Nations: The Role of Human and Social Capital* (Paris, OECD, 2001). See also the paper by one of the authors of this publication: T. Healy, 'International Evidence for the Impact of Social Capital on Well-Being', a paper to the Conference on Health Promotion and Social Capital in NUI, Galway, 28-29 June 2001.

7. I would like to acknowledge that Tom Healy, Department of Education and Science, highlighted a lack of clarity in an earlier draft of this paper relating to the conceptual framework in which indicators are utilised. To my mind there is a level of confusion and interchange between key terms, e.g. inputs, targets, etc., that does require clear differentiation. For a useful discussion of the problem see G. Palmer, 'Developing Poverty Indicators' in *Poverty Today* 51 (June/July 2001).

8. An example of inadequate distinction in these terms is illustrated in the Irish National Action Plan against Poverty and Social Inclusion 2001-

2003 where the section on indicators begins by outlining targets. See Section 4 Indicators, pp 34-36.

9. See B. Brown, 'Indicators of Child Well-Being: A Review of Current Indicators Based on Data from the Federal Statistics System' in R. M. Hauser, B.V. Brown and W.R. Prosser (eds), *Indicators of Child Well-Being* (New York, Russell Sage Foundation, 1997). See also Brown and Corbett, 'Criteria for Child Well-Being Indicators' in Annie E. Casey, *The Child Indicator: The Child Youth and Family Newsletter*, 2:6 (Winter 2001). Available on line at www.childtrends.org/ci

10. 'Criteria for Child Well-Being Indicators' in Annie E. Casey *The Child Indicator. The Child Youth and Family Newsletter*, 2:4 (Winter 2000).

11. Kristin Moore, 'Indicators of Child and Family Well-Being: The Good, the Bad, and the Ugly', an invited presentation to the National Institutes of Health, Office of Behavioural and Social Sciences, 1999 Seminar Series.

12. This summary is informed by the experience of the MONEE Project. See G. Faith, 'Regional Monitoring of Child and Family Well-being: UNICEF's MONEE project in CEE and the CIS in a Comparative Perspective'. Innocenti Working Paper, no. 72 (Florence, UNICEF Innocenti Research Centre, 2000).

13. This is a useful phrase used by Raymond Dooley, Chief Executive, Children's Rights Alliance, in his article entitled 'Creating a World Fit for Children' published in *Poverty Today*, 51 (June/July 2001), (Dublin, CPA). One of the challenges for any definition is that it must try to be open to capturing multiple horizons of growth and development and complement a personalised notion of well-being with a systemic analysis too. For example the definition proffered by the National Longitudinal Study 'as the state of children in terms of their social, psychological, physical and cognitive development' needs to be critiqued at two levels. First, whether the operating definition limits its ability to capture the multifaceted nature of development that could include spirituality? Second, whether it can assess the systemic nature of equality, discrimination, participation and best interests of the child?

14. L. Abber, 'Towards an Understanding of Children's Well-Being: Implications for Anti-Poverty Strategies' at the Combat Poverty Conference on Promoting Support for Children and Young People, Dublin Castle, July 2000. Abber is the Director of the National Centre for Children in Poverty at Columbia University, www.nccp.org.

15. Parker *et al* in M. Hill, A. Laybourn, M. Borland, Report on Well-Being – Relevant Literature – Children's Well-Being (Centre for the Study of the Child & Society, University of Glasgow, 2000), pp. 3-5.

16. K. Land, V. Lamb, S. Kahler Murillo (June 20, 2001), 'Child and Youth Well-Being in the United States 1975-1998: Some Findings from a New Index [forthcoming]'. ('An Index of Child Well Being Indicators' forthcoming in *Social Indicators Research*.)

17. Land (2001) op. cit. I have chosen not to detail the various measures identified by this research because of their specificity to the US context but will refer the reader to the original text especially pp. 7-31. (Reference relates to pagination in the pre publication manuscript.)

18. See L. Costello, *Literature Review of Child Well-Being* (Dublin, Combat Poverty Agency, 1999). Among the international studies that have identified specific indicators the following have been consulted. (1) United Nations Human Development Index is an annual study that measures the overall achievements in a country on three basic dimensions of human development – longevity, knowledge and economic resources. It is measured by life expectancy, educational attainment (adult literacy and combined primary, secondary and tertiary enrollment) and adjusted per capita income in constant purchasing power parity. (2) US Government Annual Statistical Review that led to the production of America's Children: Key National Indicators of Well-Being. The 1999 study is similar to the previous year's reports in both format and content. The selected set of indicators measure critical aspects of children's lives and are collected rigorously and regularly by Federal agencies. (3) *The Kids Count Guide on America's Youth* that led to the 11th and 12th annual *Kids Count Data Books 2000 & 2001* is a project of the Annie E. Casey Foundation. It provides a national and state-by-state effort to track the status of children in the United States. *The Kids Count Data Book* uses the best data available to measure the educational, social, economic, and physical well-being of children. (4) *The Fragile Families and Child Wellbeing Study* (FFS)1 is a longitudinal study designed to follow a new birth cohort of approximately 4,700 children, including 3,600 children born to unmarried parents. (5) *Children's Behavior and Well-Being – Findings from the National Survey of America's Families* is a snapshot produced by the Child Trends Foundation presents findings on several parent-reported measures of child well-being from the 1999 *National Survey of America's Families*

(NSAF) and compares these findings with data reported from the 1997 NSAF. These data are available for representative samples of the United States as well as for 13 states. Findings are discussed separately for adolescents and for younger children. (6) *The National Education Goals Panel Report* (NEGP) was established in July 1990 and is comprised of a bipartisan group of federal and state officials who assess and report on state and national progress toward achieving the eight National Education Goals set for the nation. (7) The UK Government is supporting a Millennium Birth Cohort Study under which 15,000 children will be included in the twelve-month period starting on 1st September 2000. (8) The US National Institute for Child Health and Human Development is sponsoring a longitudinal study of 1,200 infants sampled from hospitals in ten heterogeneous sites across America. Birth cohort studies are currently under way or in preparation in New Zealand, Canada, Germany and Sweden.

19. See the review of the Single Index of Child Well-Being Indicators in Annie E. Casey *The Child Indicator: The Child Youth and Family Newsletter*, 2:4 (Winter 2000), (Washington, Child Trends).

20. For a comprehensive example of such a mapping exercise see CERI (2001) op. cit. Appendix D 'Impact of Education in Cross-Country Regression Analysis: Some Major Studies', pp. 95-98.

21. See R. Dooley, 'Creating a World Fit for Children' in *Poverty Today*, 51 (June/July 2001).

22. www.fedgov/childstats

23. Townsend in B. Nolan and C. Whelan, *Resources, Deprivation, and Poverty* (Dublin, CPA, 1996).

24. ESRI (1998) op. cit.

25. Brink and Zeesman (1997).

26. B. Nolan, *Child Poverty in Ireland* (Dublin, Combat Poverty Agency, 1999).

27. J. Sweeney, *Ending Child Poverty in Rich Countries: What Works?* (Dublin, Children's Rights Alliance, 2001). The study quotes J. Bradshaw who stated that 'child poverty is not an inevitable result of global economic pressures or demographic transitions. Governments can and do take steps that are remarkably successful in counteracting child poverty', p. 31.

28. B. Nolan and C. Whelan, *Resources, Deprivation, and Poverty* (Dublin, CPA, 1996).

29. This was a conclusion of the New Policy institute research commissioned by the Combat Poverty Agency into the possible use of poverty indicators in the next stage of the National Anti-Poverty Strategy.

30. AEC Annual Kids Count Survey (Washington, AEC Foundation, 2001). www.aecf.org/kidcount

31. S. McLanahan and I. Garfinkel, *The Fragile Families and Child Well-Being Study* (Institute for Research on Poverty, May 2000).

32. L. Costello, *Literature Review of Child Well-Being* (Dublin, Combat Poverty Agency, 1999).

33. The YIP project was established as a response to community pressure to respond to anecdotal evidence of child prostitution in the Dundalk area that was highlighted in 1997. Support and funding from the North Eastern Health Board (NEHB) and the Peace and Reconciliation Programme (P&R) enabled an inter agency group research the situation and identify possible community based responses to the issues of young people engaged in prostitution and at risk of sexual exploitation.

34. M. Carlson, 'Do Fathers Really Matter? Father Involvement and Socio-psychological Outcomes for Adolescents', Bendheim Thomas Center for Research on Child Wellbeing Working Paper 99-04 (Princeton University, 1999).

35. Source: Eurostat, Labour Force Results 1997, Table 117, Percentage of EU households with children aged 0-18 years.

36. Eilish O'Regan in the *Irish Independent*, 20th September 2001, in response to the launch of the report on the general well-being of Irish children by the Chief Medical Officer.

37. Annual Report of the Chief Medical Officer, The Health of Our Children (Dublin, Department of Health and Children, 2000), pp. 8-9.

38. J. Micklewright and K. Stewart, 'Is Child Welfare Converging in the European Union?' EPS 69 (May 1999).

39. ESRI, The National Health and Lifestyles Surveys 1999, (Dublin: Department of Health and Children, 2000).

40. For a more detailed presentation refer to The Health of Our Children (2001), op. cit. pp. 36-48

41. P. Hogan (ed.), *Partnership and the Benefits of Learning*, pp. 67-9. (Dublin, ESAI, 1995). These papers were first presented to a symposium on philosophical issues in education policy in response to

the Minister for Education's call for dialogue and debate on the Green Paper on Education. The reference relates to a paper, 'What's the Good of Education', by Joseph Dunne who presents a good analysis of the internal goods and practices of education cf. pp. 2-78. See also Commission on the Points System Final Report and Recommendations, (Stationary Office, 1999), p. 104. In 1998 a Planning Group was established and in 1999 this group produced its Final Report and Recommendations.

42. cf. NCS (2000) op. cit. p. 19.

43. G. Palmer (April 2000) Possible Indicators of Poverty by Working Group, New Policy Institute for the Combat Poverty Agency.

44. J. Ehrle and K. Moore, 1997 'NSAF Benchmarking Measures of Child and Family Well-Being' in *Report No. 6.* (Washington DC, Urban Institute, 1999).

45. This is a concept that has been popularised and given substance by Professor Robert Putnam. See also CERI (2001) op. cit.

46. cf. NCS (2001) op. cit. pp 76-77.

47. There are a series of publications from the US that highlight the central place of community in the child's life. See J. Walsh, *The Eye of the Storm: Ten Years on the Front Line of New Future* (Baltimore, Annie E. Casey Foundation, 1999), and A. S. Bryk et al, *Improving Community School Connections* (Baltimore, Annie E. Casey Foundation, 1999).

48. cf. US Kids Count website.

49. See Objective M.

50. Innocenti Occassional Papers (1999) op. cit and 'Health and Behaviour among Young People' (WHO, 2000).

51. Ehrle and Moore (1999) op. cit.

52. Comment made in a speech by An Taoiseach, Mr Bertie Ahern T.D. at a seminar on Social Capital: Lessons for Public Policy Development at Dublin Castle, 29 March 2001 at 2.30pm. He was specifically reflecting on the National Children's Strategy and the concerns hightlighted by children in that process.

53. D. Tuohy and P. Cairns, *Youth 2K. Threat or Promise to a Religious Culture?* (Marino Institute of Education, 2000).

54. See D. Tuohy, 'The Multiple Worlds of Young People', a paper presented to the Symposium, Measuring Society: Discerning Values and Beliefs, Religion, Culture and the Social Sciences, on 23 June 2001, Maynooth College.

55. Aside from the ISSP survey there is a tradition of inquiry into belief and attitudes in Ireland. See M. NicGhiolla Phadraig (1974), A. Breslin and J. Weafer (1985), M. Mac Greil (1991) Religious Practices and Attitudes in Ireland, the European Value Systems Study 1984 and 1994 and finally *Youth 2K* (2000). Richard Kearney adverts to the fact that in a recent UNESCO questionnaire, in which there was a question: what was the most important issue of our new millennium; the majority replied: religion. See R. Kearney 'A Hermeneutics of Religion' (2000).
56. R. Kearney, *The Hermeneutics of Religion* (Indiana University Press, 2001), p. 3.